Creating Guests for Life

"Lessons learned and rules to follow for improving service"

Paul Ruby

• Chicago •

Creating Guests for Life
Paul Ruby

Contribution by: Dawn Vogelsberg

Published by
Joshua Tree Publishing
• Chicago •
JoshuaTreePublishing.com

All rights reserved. No part of this book may be reproduced or transmitted in any form or by any means, electronic or mechanical, including information storage and retrieval system without written permission from the publisher, except by a reviewer who may quote brief passages in a review.

13-Digit ISBN: 978-1-941049-87-7
Copyright © 2018. Paul Ruby. All Rights Reserved.

Photographs of Herrington Inn & Spa used with permission. Other images used with permission granted to Author.

Disclaimer:
This book is designed to provide information about the subject matter covered. The opinions and information expressed in this book are those of the author, not the publisher. Every effort has been made to make this book as complete and as accurate as possible. However, there may be mistakes both typographical and in content. Therefore, this text should be used only as a general guide and not as the ultimate source of information. The author and publisher of this book shall have neither liability nor responsibility to any person or entity with respect to any loss or damage caused or alleged to be caused directly or indirectly by the information contained in this book.

Printed in the United States of America

Dedication

This book is dedicated in memory of Eric. I will be forever grateful to my friend for hiring me at the Herrington and re-instilling my love for fishing.

Table of Contents

DEDICATION	3
TABLE OF CONTENTS	5
FOREWORD	7
SECTION 1: LESSONS LEARNED	**11**
PREFACE	13
INTRODUCTION	15
GETTING STARTED	19
"YES, BUT SHE HAS A GREAT PERSONALITY."	27
DEFINING GREAT SERVICE	33
HOTEL LIVING	37
THE RESTAURANT BUSINESS	47
LAKE SHORE	53
LESSON SUMMARY	58-59
SECTION 2: RUBY'S RULES TO FOLLOW	**61**
THE HISTORY OF THE HERRINGTON INN & SPA	63
THE HERRINGTON	65
THE MISSION	69
IS HOSPITALITY IN YOUR BLOOD?	73
FIRST AND LAST IMPRESSIONS	81
CONFLICT RESOLUTION	85
PREPARING FOR SUCCESS	99
TIME TO MAKE A CHANGE	123
RUBY'S RULES	126-127
ACKNOWLEDGMENTS	128
ABOUT THE AUTHOR	129

Foreword

When I first met Paul Ruby, he was a student at Iowa State University majoring in Hotel and Restaurant Management. I served as Department Chairman at this time and became one of Paul's instructors. His career interest in the hospitality industry was obvious to the faculty and myself during his college days.

Creating Guests for Life provides the sequence of Paul's positions and experiences in the Chicago area. After graduation, he started in an entry level position, rapidly advancing to increased professional responsibilities. Regardless of whether he served in hotels, private clubs, or restaurants, Paul's commitment is always to provide the best possible service to his guests/customers. He shares interesting examples of his guest service expectations and experiences. He has found and sincerely believes that positive guest experiences and quality products are the path to career success and satisfaction.

In addition to a busy work schedule, Paul makes time to enjoy family and other professional responsibilities. He adores his family which includes his wife Linda, two sons, Wesley who recently graduated from Iowa State University, and Logan who is an undergraduate at Iowa State University (a couple of Theta Delta Chi brothers).

As a proud alumnus, Paul served on the Iowa State University Alumni Association Board of Directors. He established the Paul Ruby Foundation for Parkinson's Research, which raised over one million dollars to support research at Northwestern University's School of Medicine.

Paul is active in his community serving on Geneva's Chamber of Commerce board of directors, the Geneva Baseball Association board of directors, and many years of coaching youth baseball.

Finally, Paul is a sports enthusiast and follows Iowa State athletics and Chicago's professional teams. He is an avid fisherman and a good golfer who won't give strokes, especially to an old worn-out faculty member.

Paul's book is a recommended resource for students majoring in hospitality management. The book would be useful in an introductory or capstone course. It could also be used in conjunction with a work experience or as an internship assignment. I am pleased that Paul is sharing his interesting and successful career.

Thomas E. Walsh, PhD

In this wonderful book, Paul Ruby shares guiding principles and simple, practical advice for anyone interested in Creating Guests for Life. He stresses the importance of setting high standards, obsessing over details, and keeping expectations crystal clear.

In today's environment, where anyone can instantly share their positive or not-so-positive experiences with thousands of people, selecting, training and developing employees is fundamental to the success of any business. Enlightened business owners understand that employees are their key competitive advantage.

As a great boss, Paul possesses both humility and strength of will. I'm fortunate to have him as a friend. Take to heart the lessons that Paul teaches in this book. Ignore them at your peril.

Rene' Boer
Author of "How to Be a Great Boss"

Paul Ruby's career has been influenced by lessons learned in the hospitality industry. This book has great significance and lessons to teach business leaders whose primary focus is creating high client expectations. Many businesses, although not in the hospitality industry, have a goal like the one Paul set for his industry, **Creating Guests for Life**.

Most businesses today focus on capturing market share by providing a unique experience for customers. They want to "create customers for life." Many industry leaders are taught that customers may not remember exactly what you do for them, but they will remember how you made them feel. Paul teaches how to best focus on the customer. If customer satisfaction is a goal, Paul's insight helps focus on the process needed to achieve such customer success no matter what the industry.

This book explains the simple behavioral lessons needed to capture and keep customers returning to the business. I have traveled all over the world and stayed in many hotels. I can say that there are only a handful that have been able to create a culture that Paul describes in **Creating Guests for Life**.

My wife and I agree that the Herrington Inn is one of our favorite hotels. We have seen in practice what Paul describes in this book. I know that the culture he has built works because we have experienced the results. Using the principles Paul shares in this book, the Herrington staff make us feel important every time we are there.

Scott Lebin RFC, CWS®

Scott Lebin, RFC, CWS®, has been working exclusively with high net worth individuals for thirty-three years. His experience as a planner and educator is sought after throughout the financial services industry. He has presented motivational seminars throughout the United States.

Section 1

Lessons Learned

This book is divided into 2 Sections. The first section focuses on the lessons learned during the first thirteen years of my career. During this period, I was doing a whole lot of learning and not much imparting of any wisdom. As I retell some of the stories I experienced, I realize how little I actually knew and how much I had to learn.

Preface

Holographic desk clerks . . . self-serving wine dispensers in the lobby bar . . . are you kidding me? Is it possible for a virtual front desk clerk to make you feel genuinely welcomed? When's the last time you received any good advice from a wine spigot?

If trendy gimmicks and automating as many tasks as possible are influencing how we define hospitality, then this book was obsolete before it was written. While improving efficiency and maximizing profit is important, we can't let these factors overshadow how critical a part the human element plays in our quest for creating guests for life. Having a longer list of amenities than our competitors may be important in regards to marketing, but "things" have little bearing on establishing customer satisfaction in comparison to what can be accomplished when a team member connects with a guest on a personal level.

> **"Amenities and trends come and go, but good service never goes out of style."**

How do we connect with our customers on a consistent basis? Hiring, training, and retaining quality employees are important, but not enough. We need to establish a culture that is so guest-centric that just thinking about our business immediately recalls feelings of complete satisfaction. This feeling results in unwavering loyalty, and hopefully, referrals.

"Ruby's Rules" began as a simple memo intended to establish basic behavioral expectations for the staff of the Herrington Inn & Spa. A few years later the mantra, "Creating guests for life," was added to clarify the overall objective and showcase examples of outstanding customer service. The stories within this book are told from the perspective of a hotel manager who has learned many lessons the hard way, but who always has the guests' best interests in mind.

This book provides insights into the hotel business as a career with anecdotes and stories, but the goal is to focus on great hospitality and creating guests for life. The concept can be translated to any business in any industry where improving customer service is important and guest loyalty is paramount. As you read this book, you will undoubtedly begin to benchmark your own customer service skills and start to develop and refine your concept of the optimal customer experience.

Introduction

I was walking with my parents and little brother on State Street in downtown Chicago when my brother yelled, "I gotta pee!" loud enough to be heard over the traffic and pedestrian noise. No worries as my dad stealthily directed our family of four through a side door, down an escalator, past a shoeshine stand where a men's room magically appeared. We were in the lower level of the Palmer House, Chicago's oldest hotel. A new tradition had just begun for the Ruby family and helped define a career path I would follow in my adulthood.

Growing up in the western suburbs of Chicago, my family would take frequent day trips into the city. We had some ritualistic behaviors. We would take the Metra train from Aurora into Union Station. After a four-block walk down Adams Street and descending a narrow flight of stairs, we would end up in the wood-paneled dining room of The Berghoff. Mixed in with a line of businessmen waiting to be seated for their two-martini lunches, we would eventually get a table. I would habitually enjoy wiener schnitzel, creamed spinach, and homemade root beer served by a veteran German waiter dressed in a white dinner jacket and black vest.

The ultimate purpose of our trips to Chicago might be shopping at Marshall Field's on State Street, visiting a museum, or attending the jazz festival at Grant Park. But it was the stop immediately following The Berghoff that dramatically impacted my future.

Palmer House Lobby

One block from the restaurant rests the iconic 1,700-room Palmer House. What started out as a "public" restroom emergency situation soon became a tradition that I looked forward to every trip. Even if we had just visited the bathroom at The Berghoff, we would venture down to the hotel's lower level restroom, where we were welcomed in the same manner as VIPs entering the front door. I couldn't wait to dig into my pocket to pull out the two quarters that I would always remember to grab from the jar on my father's dresser. I would carefully drop the coins so that they made a clinking noise loud enough for the attendant to hear when they hit the bone white plate on the vanity. Before we exited the restroom, the gracious gentleman in his spotless uniform and distinguished greying sideburns would hand me a clean cloth towel and warmly say, "Have a good day, guvna."

As I reflect on how the restroom attendant made me feel, I realize that this was someone who had the ability to create a connection that transcended well beyond his "office." He was sincere, gracious, and made a twelve-year-old kid feel important. His hospitality made a lifelong impression on me and my future.

After the bathroom stop, we would ride up the escalator to make the walk through the grand Palmer House lobby decorated with intricate murals on the ceilings, and what seemed like gold everywhere. The sights and sounds of business people checking in and out, conventioneers gathering before heading to McCormick Place, and employees helping wherever needed, created an entertaining setting for people watching. The exciting atmosphere, luxuriousness, and the hospitality received from the bathroom attendant made an everlasting impression on me. I was sold. About the sixth or seventh time making what had become a routine trek, I proudly stated to my parents at the age of twelve that "I want to work here when I grow up."

Sure enough, ten years later after obtaining a degree in Hotel and Restaurant Management, I found myself interviewing with the director of human resources at that very hotel.

My response to the question, "Why do you want to work at the Palmer House?" was a story that couldn't have been made up. Before I left the hotel with a job offer secured, I took the escalator downstairs to thank the gentleman who had made a tremendous influence on my life and probably countless others during the years he spent serving the patrons of his modest tile and porcelain domain. Although he didn't remember me from my visits as a kid, the gentleman in his crisply ironed white shirt and black bow tie was tickled by the story, and the little something extra in the grip of his handshake confirmed his appreciation for the visit.

Chapter 1

Getting Started

I had just graduated from college and was excited to be working in downtown Chicago. I was particularly thrilled to be working at the Palmer House Hilton.

Initially I was offered a food and beverage position in Hilton's management training program in Oklahoma City. I had no interest in relocating to "The Sooner State." I had my mind set on gaining experience in the front office, so I accepted an entry level front desk job at $7 per hour.

Despite missing out on a fast track opportunity, I have never regretted starting at the bottom in the front office.

Heck . . . I already had four years of experience flipping burgers at McDonald's, two as the grill supervisor. My "McSperience" included successfully handing several challenging management duties like the time I was sent out to take care of a problem on the roof of the restaurant. My friends Chris and Joe had somehow shimmied up the built-in but locked ladder on the back of the building and had been yelling my name through the exhaust hood instead of patiently waiting for me in the parking lot to get off work. I recall watching Chris dangle precariously from the "D" on the sign before falling into the bushes below, moments before the police arrived.

And when you throw in a degree in Hotel & Restaurant Management, what more could I possibly have to learn about food and beverage?

During my stint at the Palmer House, I held several positions within the front office, including a few months as the room inspector. The room inspector reconciles room status discrepancies between the front desk, housekeeping, and maintenance departments. I spent several hours each day going into rooms to confirm whether they were vacant, clean, occupied, dirty, or out of order. Despite how hard or how many times I knocked, I would occasionally find a discrepant room occupied and "in use" with guests typically too busy to notice a category four earthquake, let alone the room inspector who was sheepishly trying to sneak out of the room without being noticed. It only took one instance of inadvertently catching too much of a glimpse and then being invited in to be more than a "third wheel" for me to master the technique of properly announcing myself and giving occupants enough time to respond. This is vital if you want to avoid having some truly bizarre images permanently etched into your brain. I saw enough in three months as room inspector to not be surprised by anything on the television show *Hotel Confidential* . . . and understand why they use rubber gloves and black lights.

Lesson 1:

"Regardless of the room status, always assume the room is occupied . . .and being used."

Eventually I was promoted to the position of front desk manager, where I developed my mega convention hotel customer service skills. My skin had already begun to thicken, as one of my roles was to perform most of the walks (relocating guests with guaranteed reservations to other hotels) on oversold nights. However, I experienced a situation that was as close to being out of control as it can get. That day was a perfect storm of problems. Somehow the hotel was oversold by 400 guest rooms on a night when the entire city was sold out. To make things worse and to add a little drama, it was 40 degrees outside and pouring rain. Traffic was terrible, and everyone seemed to be in a bad mood. The result was a ten-hour shift of non-stop stress, confusion, and mass guest dissatisfaction.

Imagine a line of guests wrapped around a Chicago city block in the rain, waiting for almost an hour to check in to their hotel. Most of these cold, wet, and increasingly impatient people had arrived at O'Hare airport several hours earlier and endured a ninety-minute bumper-to-bumper taxi ride into the city. My mission on this day, with 1,100 arrivals and only 700 vacant rooms, was to decide which lucky guests would get to stay, and who would be receiving $50 for cab fare and a hotel voucher for their surprise stay back at the O'Hare Hilton.

I have always been at ease confronting disgruntled guests without taking things personally, but on this particular day, I was glad to stay anonymous behind the safety of a one-way mirror. This was markedly true as I watched two security officers rushing over to remove one of the many less-than-satisfied patrons who, with the lobby full of soaking wet and frustrated people, jumped up on the front desk. He was wearing a trench coat, and I fully expected him to whip open is coat and flash the frustrated mob waiting to check in. Instead he screamed at the top of his lungs, "Don't bother waiting in line—they don't have any f$#%ng rooms!"

After eight straight hours of listening to guests insisting and begging to be given rooms, my thick skin could have made an elephant jealous. Unfortunately, what should have been a teaching moment to show the importance of empathy and demonstrate the power of making things right in adverse situations was simply reduced to survival for the staff—and guest retention be damned.

Lesson 2:

"You won't last long if you take things too personally."

Creating Guests for Life

Everybody makes mistakes. It's typically how we react when we become aware of the problem that determines a guest's impression.

I was at my desk when one of the desk clerks came back to tell me that Andre Dawson wanted to speak with me because he was unhappy with the room he was assigned. Before I went out front to meet the newly acquired Chicago Cubs player, I looked in the property management system to see what room he was checked into. I realized immediately why the slugging right fielder was unhappy. This was not a good way to begin his first season in Chicago, as he had been checked into what we called a "New York Overnight." The room was so small that the lamp and alarm clock had to be bolted to a small shelf on the wall because there was no room for a night stand. I tried to imagine the six-foot three future hall of famer with his feet dangling off the end of the twin bed in a room that didn't even have a television.

I went out to the front desk to meet him and apologized for our mistake before he had a chance to tell me what was wrong. I quickly changed his room to a suite, apologized again, called a bellman, and handed him a new key to assist with moving his luggage. The entire transaction took no more than two minutes. Mr. Dawson was exhausted and just wanted to relax.

I then gave him enough time to get to his room and unpack before calling to make sure his new accommodations were suitable, apologize again, and ask if he needed anything else. My objective was to make things right and follow up to confirm, rather than assume he was happy with the room change and make sure there was nothing else I could do to make his stay more enjoyable. He was very appreciative for the quick response and asked for my name.

I wasn't sure why he wanted my name until the next day when an envelope was delivered to me with two front row tickets to that afternoon's game. I had managed to make a positive out of a negative by inadvertently selecting the one suite in the hotel with a pool table in the parlor, not knowing he was an avid pool player. Although I would have followed the same procedure if Andre had been traded to the White Sox, being a lifelong Cubs fan may have influenced the level of his room upgrade slightly.

Lesson 3:

"Following up, being prompt, and attentive service is appreciated, and sometimes throwing in a pool table doesn't hurt."

One of the challenges of working in a large convention hotel is the "cattle call" mentality. The sheer volume of transactions challenges the staff's ability to connect with guests in a way that would establish loyalty. Smaller hotels typically have the advantage of a higher ratio of employees per room and less dependency on large groups, which lowers the percentage of repeat guests. However, regardless of the size, market segment, brand or location of a hotel, the factor that almost always has the most influence on guest satisfaction is the actions or inactions of the staff.

Although I enjoyed the challenge and thrill of solving big problems in a big hotel, I began to realize that big hotels are typically departmentalized, making it difficult to gain exposure to other departments. I still had plenty to learn, but I was impatient, and my experience was not as diversified as I wanted it to be.

I also did some basic math and determined that my income had gone the wrong direction when I was promoted to the front desk manager and became a salaried employee. Prior to my promotion I was making $7.25 an hour plus overtime, working 65 hours per week at a salary of $15,000. I was now making less than $5 per hour.

When I was offered the position of evening manager at the Drake Oakbrook Hotel at a salary of $18,000, I thought I had hit the jackpot.

The Drake Oakbrook

Chapter 2

"Yes, but she has a great personality."

Soon after I arrived at the Drake, I was promoted from evening manager to front office manager. A few months later, the director of housekeeping was terminated, and I offered to take over the housekeeping department in addition to my front office duties. I was anxious to learn everything I could and accept as much responsibility as my boss would allow me to take on. In my spare time I started making "cold calls" to assist the sales department.

I was very fortunate to be under the wing of Dave Flando, the general manager, who continues to mentor me to this day. I appreciate Dave now, and I really appreciated him when he recommended me to the owner to be his successor when he left the Drake to accept a position at a larger hotel in Chicago.

In addition to my assertiveness and Dave's grooming, I realize now I was also fortunate to have an aggressively receding hairline. I'm pretty sure the owner did not realize that I was only twenty-five-years-old when I was handed the reins. But I was confident and with my McDonald's experience, a year and a half at a large convention hotel, and two years at the Drake under my belt, surely I knew everything I needed to know to be successful.

Lesson 4:

"Bald is beautiful...especially when it makes you look older and more experienced than you really are."

The Drake Oakbrook opened in 1962 as Chicagoland's premier suburban hotel. Unfortunately, when I arrived in the late 1980s, very little had been reinvested into the property since it opened—and it showed. The hotel had several excellent long-time employees, but the combination of other new hotel options and the worn feel of the Drake made it increasingly difficult to attract new guests and clients. The hotel was still operating without a property management system. Reservations were typed by hand and placed in buckets.

This chapter could also be titled:

"If the property can't compare physically with the competition, you better have the right people in place providing great service."

The physical challenges of the facility created a situation where the success of the hotel was almost completely dependent on its reputation going back to when the hotel was associated with Drake Chicago, and the service provided by some key staff members—the cast of characters who did everything they could to keep the hotel competitive.

"Mr. Catering"—Gino was 100% Italian and his old-world charm, accent, knowledge of the business and relentless work ethic combined to create one of the most famous catering directors in the Chicago area. He could schmooze future brides and their mothers better than anyone I have ever met. I'm sure he told at least a thousand brides, "You are the most beautiful bride I have ever seen." His other standby line was to make the "mistake" of referring to the bride's mother as her sister. Gino's ability to remember names and faces was uncanny and served him and the Drake Oak Brook well during his five decades at the property.

"Crazy Mo"—Although acceptable office decorum in the mid-1980s had come a long way from the *Mad Men* days, there were plenty of crazy things going on. Petty personnel issues during my time at the Drake would undoubtedly be considered legal nightmares now. Mo was our human resources director, who did an amazing job keeping the hotel out of trouble with the departments of labor, immigration, and probably several other government entities. She instilled in me the importance of documentation and treating staff consistently. Most importantly, she taught me the importance of keeping things in perspective and having fun. Mo also knew how critical it was to retain quality team members and the financial and emotional costs it takes to replace them.

"Chef Klaus"—Our Austrian chef was literally just off the boat. His previous job was on a cruise ship, and like Gino, Klaus used his ethnicity and accent to his advantage. Klaus was confident and made it clear he knew more than I did about anything culinary. Klaus was the kind of chef everyone wanted to know. He was exuberant, charismatic, and said what was on his mind. Klaus would do something as simple as bring out the amuse bouche to the table or make more of a spectacle like flambéing a dessert table-side with an exotic liquor. Whatever he did, he did with pizazz and kept the guests coming back.

"Lovely Linda"—Although Linda took a different approach than Gino, Linda truly understood the importance of connecting with clients. She had a difficult property to sell, but Linda was adept at becoming friends with most of the key meeting planners and admins who booked rooms in the area. She had the gift of making her clients loyal to her rather than to the property, which was important based on the physical issues with the hotel. Linda was also known to her clients as quite simply the most fun person in the room and had the knack for drawing in the people around her. Linda and I have been married to each other since 1994, and she is still the life of the party.

"Grandma Alice"—Alice finally retired in her mid-80s, but while at the Drake, she was everyone's grandmother, including guests, employees, and vendors. She attempted to simultaneously take care of everyone while receiving and transferring calls as the full-time switchboard operator. Although it was common for her to leave someone on hold for extended periods of time, she was undoubtedly attempting to do something to make someone else happy. Alice was unfortunately almost entirely deaf, suffered from irritable bowel syndrome, and was a little forgetful . . . not ideal characteristics for a switchboard operator. But she had a way of making up for her challenges by being able to sense over the phone when a guest was sick and having a bowl of chicken soup ready for them at check-in.

"Johnny Iknowaguy"—If you needed anything, Johnny, the bell captain, had a way of making it happen. There were the typical requests like restaurant reservations, limos, and directions, but Johnny was connected and "knew a guy" for everything. He made a sound living getting groups into VIP rooms at the trendiest nightclubs, finding companions for businessmen, and always having a hot tip for guests wanting to bet the ponies. If Johnny couldn't acquire an item for you, you probably shouldn't have asked in the first place.

"Lafonda"—Lafonda was a gold-toothed room attendant from a rough neighborhood on the west side of Chicago. If you put a helmet on her head, she could have easily been mistaken for a defensive end on the Chicago Bears. But if you got to know Lafonda, you knew she would do anything for you and was the most requested room attendant by our regular guests. Although I don't think she could make an elephant out of a hand towel like on a cruise ship if her life depended on it, she took her job seriously and never compromised her attention to detail. She was friendly, thoughtful, and appreciative to every guest she encountered.

Added to this unique collection of characters was a receiving clerk who was rumored to provide gigolo services, a beverage manager with a drinking problem, a chief engineer on the take, an aloof restaurant manager, a voluptuous secretary whose second job was making "movies," and a twenty-five-year-old general manager who was out over his skis. I had a recipe for a sitcom that would rival *Fawlty Towers*. Somehow, despite of the building being in desperate need of a renovation, and the quirkiness of the staff, guests kept coming back. The sincere desire to please each and every guest overshadowed countless physical deficiencies.

Chapter 3

Defining Great Service

What is good service? When guest expectations are low, and we exceed them... not too exciting. But when guest expectations are high, and we manage to do even better, then we have accomplished something.

In order to be able to seize every opportunity to do the things that help to create guests for life, we first must be able to identify those opportunities. Being aware of what is going on around us at the moment—and knowing what is going to happen in the future—helps.

A guest may refuse assistance with their luggage as they struggle to carry their bags up the stairs, but this does not mean we can't run up the stairs ahead of the guests to open the door for them. What is the alternative? Watch the guest carry their bags and then open the door for themselves.

Our focus and mindset must be "What can I do to make a positive impression on every guest that I come in contact with?" It takes initiative, anticipation, caring, and sometimes a little hustle.

When you recall your most memorable hotel, dining, or other hospitality-related experience, what is the first thing that comes to mind? Is it the room, the view, or the food?

When I think of memorable all-around top service experiences, the first one that I can recall happened soon after I was promoted to general manager. I was headed on a vacation to Florida with a buddy. The owner of the hotel arranged for us to play golf at The Jupiter Hills Club. Knowing it was ranked in Golf Magazine's top 100 courses, I had high expectations and was looking forward to playing.

You only have one chance to make a first impression, and boy, did the Jupiter Hills Club get off to a great start. To this day I am not entirely sure how they pulled it off, but when we arrived at the security guard station and I rolled down the window of the rented minivan, I was immediately made to feel important when the guard said, "Welcome, Mr. Ruby, to Jupiter Hills," as if he had been anxiously waiting to meet a celebrity. My buddy and I shrugged our shoulders and without saying a word we both knew that this was going to be an excellent day.

The staff seemed to sense we were out of our element and anticipated our every need. We were then escorted to the bag drop where an attendant opened my door and again greeted me by name. The attendant took our bags, the valet took care of the van, and a locker room attendant said, "Please follow me, Mr. Ruby," and brought us to our lockers, which of course had our names on them. We were then escorted up to the pro shop, greeted by name by one of the golf pros and then introduced to our fore caddie who took us to the first tee.

We finished playing the front-nine, and we were just starting to get used to our caddies doing everything except actually hitting our balls for us . . . (However, out of mercy, I think my caddie used a wedge when he thought no one was looking so I would avoid an impossible shot). We were instructed that it was time for lunch.

A table was already reserved for Mr. Ruby, and the hostess acted like she had known me for years. Every staff person I encountered was not only polite and proactive; they also seemed to genuinely enjoy making two twenty-something average Joes from Chicago, who were not members, feel special.

The service afforded us was unforced, and providing hospitality, was clearly more than just part of their job. Every staff member seemed to have put themselves in our golf shoes and knew how to make two regular guys feel like rock stars for a day. The bottom line is I have no idea what my score was that day, or if played well or poorly. I can't even remember anything about the course aside from I am pretty sure there were more hills than usual in Florida—and I have no idea what I had for lunch.

But the one thing I will never forget about that day was how the staff made me feel. Almost thirty years later, I can think back to my day at The Jupiter Hills Club when I need an example of what I consider to be great service.

Lesson 5:

"Guests may not remember your name, what they ate or details about their stay, but if you have done your job well, they will not forget how you made them feel."

Chapter 4

Hotel Living

It is difficult if not impossible to effectively manage people if you never leave your desk. It is vital that you inspect what you expect. Walking around also helps you to see what our customers see and most importantly keeps employees "on their toes."

The owner of the Drake asked me if I would consider living at the hotel. I jumped at the chance to reduce my housing costs and shorten my commute down to about 30 seconds. The perks were wonderful, with someone to clean my suite, wash my clothes, and cook my food. The situation had its downside though, as my privacy was compromised, and I was never actually off work. My phone could ring at any time of the day or night to deal with rowdy wedding guests or more serious problems such as the occasional crime or death.

I was called to the restaurant for an emergency situation on a busy Friday night. When I arrived in the dining room, the restaurant manager explained that he had already called 911, and that it appeared that an older gentleman in a party of eight had a heart attack. As I approached the group that had gathered around a man lying on the floor in the middle of the dining room, I was dumbfounded by the inaction of the visibly distraught people just standing around. I jumped into action and attempted to take control and implement my recently acquired CPR certification skills. I began barking orders and asked the group to move back so I could kneel down to begin administering CPR. It was about this time that someone from the group tugged on my suit jacket to pull me away from the family member who was about to die. I then noticed he was wearing a hospital bracelet with the letters DNR, and the situation began to make some sense. Within a few minutes, the paramedics arrived, placed the man on a gurney, and took him away by ambulance.

The piano player resumed playing, but with a much more somber repertoire, and was performing to a much smaller audience as most diners had lost their appetite and many left without paying. Sometimes trying to exceed a guest's expectations can backfire.

I took a look at the reservation book to find out the name of the party of eight and saw the comment "special occasion—see Sue for details."

Sue worked with the daughter of the guest of honor to plan the dinner party and asked questions in an attempt to make sure no detail was forgotten. She ended up ordering a custom cake and a centerpiece and found out the guest of honor's favorite song for the piano player to play when the group arrived. She also reserved the best table in the house, which happened to be in the middle of the dining room. What Sue forgot to ask was, "What was the special occasion?" It turns out that the guest of honor was terminally ill and wanted to dine with his family at his favorite restaurant one last time.

Lesson 6:

"If guests are coming in for a special reason, find out what the occasion is, and if it is for a "last supper," put them in the back room."

Just as walking around is necessary to keep an eye on the staff, we also need to be visible to our guests if we expect to connect with them.

Living at the hotel afforded me more contact with guests, in particular during the late evening when most general managers would be home. I had become friendly with one of our regular VIPs who lived just west of the city and reserved a hospitality suite on a regular basis. The bellman knew to always notify me when this impeccably dressed sixty-something guest valeted his Cadillac so I could personally greet him and his entourage at check-in. He usually had one or more pretty women near him and tipped the staff like he was printing money.

Every time I saw him, he would ask if I was ready to take him up on his offer to send his tailor over to fit me for a new suit. I would have looked great in a fine Italian wool suit, but I never got fitted or accepted any cash tips. Despite my inexperience, I had already developed a healthy sense of ethics and something didn't seem quite right. However, I was still very surprised when I received a subpoena from the U.S. Attorney requiring registration cards and any other information the hotel had on the guest from Cicero. I was concerned about breaching guest confidentiality, but I was assured by the U.S. Attorney that I was not in jeopardy of compromising any laws or ethical obligations, so I provided the subpoenaed information and arrived at the courthouse as instructed. I had no idea why I was being asked to testify, and I didn't think much of it until the U.S. Attorney uttered the phrase, "Don't feel intimidated during your cross examination . . . Remember, you have done nothing wrong."

I breezed through the prosecutor's questions thinking it was kind of fun going through the process of being a witness. I remember sitting in the witness chair and thinking that it must have been an important case based on all the reporters, television stations, and general public who had filled the courtroom. However, any sense of having fun quickly changed into an uncomfortable nervousness once the defense attorney started his cross examination.

All I was doing was verifying what information was captured on a registration card and basic procedures for checking in and checking out guests. I was already a bit confused and concerned from the "don't feel intimidated" comment from the U.S. Attorney. If the defense attorney's job is to make witnesses uneasy or trick them into saying what the defense team wants to hear, this guy was good. Based on the defense attorney's line of questioning, it seemed like I was being accused of doing something wrong. When he raised his voice as if he was reprimanding me, I began to wonder what I had gotten myself into. I made it through the cross examination with a minimal amount of stammering and without any mistakes. I was thanked by the U.S. Attorney, dismissed and allowed to go home.

It wasn't until the next day when I read the newspaper that I realized why he had always registered under an alias. I had just testified against a notorious mobster. Little did I know that the gentleman who I thought was just a stressed-out businessman living in the fast lane had actually been operating a gambling ring in one of the hotel's hospitality suites. Lucky for me, my connected friend had bigger fish to fry as his chauffeur had made a plea deal and ratted out his boss for a murder rap for what the mobster referred to as "trunk music." I was relieved that I didn't have to enter the witness protection program and move to Boise, Idaho. In the end a guest for life was created . . . it just happened to be in a different kind of facility.

Lesson 7:

"Always be friendly but be careful who you befriend."

Being a new general manager, I experienced a number of firsts at the Drake, including my first union negotiation. When I answered the telephone call from the local union representative asking to meet, I wasn't sure what to expect. I knew the housekeeping and banquet departments were members of the union, but I was unclear about what influence the union had with the hotel. I was "winging it" as the two slightly intimidating gentlemen sat down in my office. After some brief small talk, one of them handed me a list of "demands" scribbled on a napkin. Not knowing quite how to respond, I excused myself to talk with the owner, who had an office at the hotel.

As soon as I timidly handed my boss the list of demands, and before he even read what was scribbled on the napkin, he said, "Tell him you are prepared to close the hotel, and he can shove this up his ass." as he handed back a now wadded up napkin. I returned to the bargaining table instilled with some confidence when I realized if things went south, I was just following directions. I left out the part about what they could do with their cocktail napkin, but I made it crystal clear that we wouldn't be agreeing to any base wage increases or changes to the insurance plan. The entire meeting lasted no more than five minutes and the outcome was just as the owner knew it would be. The hotel remained open, and no employees walked off the job or picketed—and on the surface, it looked like I knew what I was doing.

Lesson 8:

"It's important to understand who has leverage and show confidence even if you have to fake it."

I also did some of the best crime fighting of my career while at the Drake. It was about ten o'clock one night when a distraught female guest asked to meet me in the lobby. She explained that she had just come back from a dinner meeting, and she was convinced someone had gone through her suitcase and stole some of her underwear. We were both a little embarrassed, and after half-heartedly taking some notes of when the alleged theft took place and a description of what was missing, I assured the guest, who might have been a little tipsy, that I would investigate the situation and get back to her. I had experienced enough false accusations of housekeeping staff stealing things from rooms that I suspected that the guest had inadvertently left the underwear at home and would eventually be calling me to apologize for her mistake. That was until I received a second complaint about missing underwear, and then another woman found someone else's underwear in her suitcase . . . and they kept coming.

Fortunately, as I did with the first occurrence, I documented the date, time, and other details of each subsequent incident, which now added up to over a dozen incidents over a three-month period.

It was obvious that the growing problem was being perpetrated by an employee who either wanted to be caught . . . or couldn't control his need to escalate the bizarreness of the fetish. I developed a matrix that included incident dates combined with employee schedules, with the hope of narrowing down suspects. Eventually the evidence clearly pointed to a young houseman.

I then enlisted the help of the Oakbrook police department to develop a plan to catch the thief red-handed. The houseman was radioed to clean up a spill in one of the entrance vestibules. As he was mopping up the mess, an attractive woman walked by with a suitcase and entered a nearby guest room. She then dropped off her suitcase in the room, walked past the houseman again, got in her car and drove off. The chief of police was in my office with me when a voice on his radio crackled emphatically "We got him!" As soon as the female guest had got in her car, the houseman had entered her room. He emerged a few minutes later and was immediately greeted by a police officer who had been watching through the peephole of the room across the hall.

Nothing aside from Miranda rights needed to be said as the employee was caught "pink handed" with a pair of lacy underwear in his grasp before he was able to stuff them down his pants. The frightened and embarrassed employee was handcuffed and taken to the municipal jail where, when questioned, admitted to having stolen underwear from over twenty women, several of whom were too embarrassed to let anyone know or to make a claim.

It was a great feeling to solve the crime, and I was glad to call the victims to explain what had happened. However, despite the apparent success, I highly doubt any of the victims ever returned to the Drake, let alone became guests for life.

Lesson 9:

"Take every guest complaint seriously even if it sounds far-fetched. And never underestimate the weird things people are capable of doing."

A newspaper reporter found out I was living in the hotel and asked if she could write a story about what it was like to be a hotel manager who lived on site. I agreed to the interview, thinking I could focus some attention on the hotel's attributes and gain some good publicity. In hindsight, the reporter had an angle she was trying to convey in the story. She kept asking me questions such as, "If you wanted to have a dinner party for six in your suite served by the restaurant staff, could you?" and "Are all of the amenities of the hotel such as the pool and sauna at your disposal?" My response was the same for each question: "Yes, but I haven't and wouldn't."

She also wanted me to tell her about any interesting experiences that could be attributed to my living in the hotel. I decided I probably shouldn't bring up the panty raider story, or when I found a houseman asleep late at night on one of the rollaway beds in an empty office. I also neglected to mention that she might have been able to shoot some craps in a suite if the interview would have taken place a few months earlier. I did mention how I had more of an opportunity to meet guests and get to know many of the regular guests. I explained how rewarding it was to be able to personally provide service when most other general managers were home.

The article was published with a picture of me in front of the hotel and the headline "Hotel Living." Despite my qualifying response of yes, but I haven't and wouldn't, the entire focus was on all of the lavish amenities and services I had available to me. I had never even thought about taking a dip in the pool or using the sauna. But according to the article, the twenty-something year old bachelor had a chef at his personal disposal, room service any time he wanted, the key to the wine cellar, an indoor pool to cool off in, and a sauna to warm him up. I came across as a pompous ass that lived a lavish lifestyle. Fortunately, the owner knew the truth, but it took some time for the ribbing from my friends and colleagues to stop. I learned the hard way to insist on approval before agreeing to being interviewed.

Lesson 10:

"Retain the right to proof before going to print."

Chapter 5

The Restaurant Business

Prior to moving into the hotel, I was living in an apartment above a restaurant in the Lincoln Park neighborhood of Chicago. I enjoyed getting to know Dino, the owner, and became friends with the always-cheerful Albanian immigrant restaurateur. Dino was constantly looking for new deals, investors, and partners. For some reason he thought I had some money and was always pitching me "once-in-a-lifetime opportunities."

It had been about a year since I had moved into the hotel, and I hadn't communicated with Dino for a few months. He called me and explained that he had a deal all worked out for a restaurant space in Lincoln Park, but he was spread too thin to manage it by himself. He needed a partner. I reluctantly agreed to take a look at the site and the proposed lease. The available space was located within a building once owned by Al Capone and was directly across the street from the Lincoln Park Zoo. The location, size, rent, and build-out allowance seemed too good to be true, but after my attorney reviewed the details with me and even he was tempted to invest, I decided to take the plunge. I worked out an exit strategy with the owner of the Drake, and before I knew what hit me, I was swinging a sledge hammer and making way for a new white tablecloth Italian restaurant within earshot of the barking sea lions and howling wolves. Ruby's On the Park was born.

"Take the plunge" would prove to be an understatement as within sixty days of signing the deal for the Ruby's site, Dino and I had worked out two additional restaurant deals. My new partner had found a real estate investment company that was buying downtown high-rise apartment buildings and converting them into condos. Two of the buildings contained restaurants that were insignificant components of the multi-million-dollar real estate deals. However, the building owner was anxious to get out of the restaurant business, as the manager they employed was robbing them blind, and the operations were hemorrhaging cash. After working out unquestionably favorable lease deals, we were literally handed the keys and given the combination to the safe that was still filled with several days of cash receipts, petty cash, and a loaded handgun.

Things were quickly spiraling out of control and getting very complicated. To simplify our business arrangement, Dino and I eventually decided to split up our "restaurant empire," leaving me with the Lincoln Park location, which was still under construction. Designing and building a restaurant from scratch entails many daunting tasks, but nothing compares to the nightmare of obtaining a liquor license in the city of Chicago.

With help from a guy in a small office in the lower level of city hall, I learned "the Chicago way" of how things get done. One of my first tasks after signing the lease was to hire an architect to lay out the restaurant space and create mechanical drawings. The plans had been submitted with my building permit application, which needed to be approved before I could obtain a liquor license. However, they kept getting kicked back to me with a "denied" stamp and some illegible scribbles supposedly explaining what I was missing. After numerous trips to city hall and being bounced around from one department to another, I finally found someone in the city building department who was able to help. Although he was careful not to say out loud how things work, I eventually figured out that the phrase, "highly recommend you utilize a different architect" is code for "you need to use his guy if you want to avoid continued delays." I reluctantly accepted the business card of an architect who I was assured would expedite the approval process.

The arrangement was of course a cash-only deal, and after handing over the envelope for drawings that cost me twice as much as the original plans, and yet inferior in detail, I whisked through the approval process as promised. I found out later that the person who prepared the approved plans was not even a licensed architect. He was still working on his degree, but more importantly, he was the nephew of someone high up in the city building department.

Lesson 11:

"You can't fight city hall."

The restaurant was finally ready for a pre-opening party. I was starting to have a better understanding of how things worked in Chicago, and I made sure to send invitations to every politician or city employee I could think of who could influence the success or failure of my business. After a successful night of giving the house away to what seemed like every freeloader on this side of the Mississippi, Ruby's On the Park opened to the public.

If you can't comprehend the importance of creating guests for life when your own money is on the line, you never will.

In a city with thousands of restaurants and plenty of them teetering between success and failure, every day required relentless focus on doing whatever was within my control to remain competitive. I was extremely conscientious about providing a warm greeting to every guest as they walked in, and a genuine thank-you on their way out. If they made a reservation or paid by credit card, I would call them by name. My goal was to create a "neighborhood" restaurant where the patrons felt like Ruby's On the Park was to them what *Cheers* was to Norm and Cliff in Boston.

Former Illinois governor James "Big Jim" Thompson served as the "guest of honor" at the pre-opening party and lived in the penthouse next door. He came in for dinner at least once a week. I was careful not to treat him differently than the other patrons. He would be appreciated, but not coddled. The staff and I would be attentive but hopefully in the same manner that we treated all our customers.

The objective was to make every guest feel like they were the governor. I tried to instill in the staff that anyone who walked through the door could be a potential big-spending regular, or even a restaurant critic, so treat everyone as a VIP.

Based on two reviews we received soon after opening, it was clear that the staff "got it." One critic stated, "The staff was attentive without hovering" and "We were made to feel special from the moment we walked in the door until we left."

Despite excellent reviews and a growing base of regular patrons, the challenges of being a restaurant owner never seemed to let up.

I attempted to be aware of and control everything that influenced my customers' impressions of the restaurant. It took a while before I realized that customers didn't care whether a problem was not my fault or out of my control. A negative experience—regardless of the circumstances—often results in the loss of a customer. The key to minimizing the number of customers who fall into this category is not always within our control or as easy as it might appear.

Parking is a nightmare in the Lincoln Park neighborhood of Chicago, and I contracted with a valet company to provide a much-needed service for our guests. Unfortunately, valet parkers have been known to be missing a scruple or two. Every now and then I would hear from customers who had received parking tickets on nights when they had dined at the restaurant. The valet parkers would roll the dice and park in no-parking zones and in front of water hydrants. If the valet found a parking ticket when they went to retrieve the car, they would throw it out, knowing it would be several weeks or months later before the guest would be notified by mail of their infraction.

Although I would reimburse the guest for the cost of the ticket, and in turn get reimbursed by the valet company, a bad impression was left that may have overshadowed what could have otherwise been a great experience.

Lesson 12:

"It takes more than just making things right to retain a customer let alone to create a customer for life."

Although I had two years left on my lease, my landlord had a prospective tenant who was willing to pay a higher rent and purchase the kitchen equipment and furnishings from me. With only twelve days off during the previous three years and not much money saved, the chance to get out of my lease early was a relatively easy decision.

Despite having little to show for my efforts, save for several life lessons and an appreciation of the value of parking spaces in Lincoln Park, I was able to get out of the restaurant business relatively unscathed. After starting from scratch and operating Ruby's On the Park for three years, surely I knew everything there was to know about the restaurant business . . .

Chapter 6

Lake Shore

One of my former regular guests at Ruby's found out I was leaving the restaurant business and asked if I was interested in an opportunity at the country club at which he was a member. Despite not having any previous private club experience, I was very fortunate to be offered the assistant general manager position at Lake Shore Country Club. Located in the north shore suburb of Glencoe, it's one of the most prestigious private country clubs in the Midwest.

I quickly learned how much I didn't know about refined service. I received condescending glares from Mary, the red-headed dining room manager, for my ignorance. She was impatient, and her temper was as fiery as her hair. But I soon realized she was good at her job, and if we didn't kill each other first, she could teach me a lot.

On the other end of the patience spectrum was Henry, the club's long-time general manager. He taught me to leave nothing to chance, and the importance of contingency plans. Henry had the patience of a saint. He is also humble, gracious, frugal, and his unwavering sense of ethics made him a perfect fit for the blue-blooded members at Lake Shore. He remains a trusted confidant and mentor to this day.

Henry and I worked together planning several beautiful wedding receptions and other events until he knew I was ready to work directly with the member or committee on my own. He taught me the importance of attention to detail and what questions to ask to ensure nothing was left to chance. Who, what, and when details down to the timing in fifteen-minute increments were included on the banquet event order. Every staff member would be able to look at the banquet event order to see that Javier was to be setting up tables and chairs from 4-5:00 p.m., on dinner break from 5-5:30 p.m., valeting cars from 5:30-6:30 p.m., passing hors d' oeuvres from 6:30 p.m. (including what food he was passing), servicing tables 3 and 4 during dinner, and then back to valet from 8:00 p.m. until all cars were gone. The details made it easy to manage the staff, and more importantly, ensure that everything flowed and was executed exactly how the member envisioned it would happen.

Menu details would include portion sizes, sauces, garnishes, and a picture of how the food should be arranged on the plate. Glassware, tableware, table cloth, and napkin details were also included. Outdoor events would have bad weather plans with multiple options based on wind, rain, temperature, etc.

Lesson 13:

"If in doubt, write it out."

I learned about anticipation. We typically would know which members were to be expected for dinner or for events, but we would take things several steps further. The cars of the members, and sometimes even some of their guests, were memorized. As we would see their cars entering the front gate of the club, we would begin preparing their usual drink so it would be waiting for them when they entered the front door.

The legendary broadcaster, Jack Brickhouse, was one of my boyhood idols as the voice of the Chicago Cubs from 1948–1981. He endured a lot of mediocre teams during those thirty-four seasons; yet, he always remained optimistic with his celebratory phrase "Hey hey." Jack was a regular guest of one of the members. It was always a good feeling to see the smile on the host's face and obvious pride when we had Mr. Brickhouse's Dewar's and water with two ice cubes and a twist waiting for him as he exited his Buick sedan.

Lesson 14:

"Anticipation is an important part of exceeding guests' expectations."

The importance of smiling could probably be reiterated in every chapter, but if I had to select one person on earth that truly exemplifies the impact a smile can make, it would be Gertrude. Gertie grew up on the small West Indie island of Dominica. While I am quite certain she came out of the womb smiling, I think she perfected her ability to make everyone around her a little happier with her positive attitude and pearly whites after immigrating to Chicago.

Gertie was a nanny for one of the member families at Lake Shore but was becoming obsolete with her charges now in high school. The moment anyone meets Gertie, they can feel her warmth and sincere desire to please . . . and her smile, sometimes, is accompanied with a mischievous grin that exudes friendliness.

Twenty-three years after I hired Gertie, she is still pleasing the members at Lake Shore and has never stopped smiling. I have witnessed an elderly woman change from being angry and berating a busboy seemingly with the goal of bringing him to tears to being calm and thankful due to only the magic of Gertie's smile and positive reassurance.

Gertie was not only able to satisfy the customer but also retain the busboy who would have probably quit if not for her intervention. And if Gertie forgot a garnish for a drink, or didn't remember what the soup du jour was, no one could be angry with the woman that was seemingly always happy to be doing what she was doing wherever she was at the moment . . . according to her smile.

Lesson 15:

"Never underestimate the power of a smile."

I truly enjoyed my job at Lake Shore, but I had become impatient and felt ready for a general manager position, and I applied for positions in the club industry and the hotel business. I found myself in a quandary as I ended up with two job offers.

One was at a well-respected private country club on the North shore of Chicago and the other was at a small hotel that had opened up six years earlier in Geneva, Illinois.

Although on the surface the opportunity at The Herrington Inn seemed like it might not be very challenging, it was explained that the owner was in the process of adding a meeting and banquet facility and a twenty-three-room addition to the property, and they needed someone with my experience to manage the expanding business.

What wasn't explained to me was the incredible turnover the hotel had battled since the property had opened, and the desperate need for someone to come in and stabilize the situation. Coincidentally, my wife and I had had dinner at the hotel the month prior, and I grew up just a few miles to the south of Geneva.

Although the club position paid more, I was intrigued by the opportunity in Geneva and made the decision to return to the hotel industry.

Lesson Summary

Lesson 1:
"Regardless of the room status, always assume the room is occupied . . . and being used."

Lesson 2:
"You won't last long if you take things too personally."

Lesson 3:
"Following up, being prompt, and attentive service is appreciated, and sometimes throwing in a pool table doesn't hurt."

Lesson 4:
"Bald is beautiful...especially when it makes you look older and more experienced than you really are."

Lesson 5:
"Guests may not remember your name, what they ate or details about their stay, but if you have done your job well, they will not forget how you made them feel."

Lesson 6:
"If guests are coming in for a special reason, find out what the occasion is, and if it is for a "last supper," put them in the back room."

Lesson 7:
"Always be friendly but be careful who you befriend."

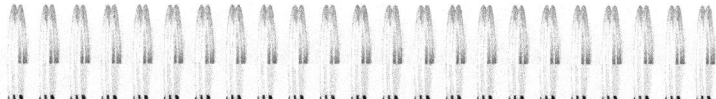

Lesson Summary

Lesson 8:
"It's important to understand who has leverage and show confidence even if you have to fake it."

Lesson 9:
"Take every guest complaint seriously even if it sounds far-fetched. And never underestimate the weird things people are capable of doing."

Lesson 10:
"Retain the right to proof before going to print."

Lesson 11:
"You can't fight city hall."

Lesson 12:
"It takes more than just making things right to retain a customer let alone to create a customer for life."

Lesson 13:
"If in doubt, write it out."

Lesson 14:
"Anticipation is an important part of exceeding guests' expectations."

Lesson 15:
"Never underestimate the power of a smile."

Section 2

Ruby's Rules to follow.

Although we never stop learning, at some point I realized that I had experienced my share of lessons— and it was time to put them to good use. Stories had evolved into Lessons. Lessons were turned into rules. And rules then became the premise for the Section 2 of this book.

The History of the Herrington Inn & Spa

Twenty-five years ago, a luxurious forty-room inn with a fine dining restaurant opened along the west bank of the Fox River where a dilapidated building once stood in downtown Geneva. The property was named the Herrington Inn when it opened in 1993.

The site was originally the homestead of Geneva's first settlers, James and Charity Herrington, who arrived from Philadelphia back in 1835. In 1874, a small creamery was built on the site utilizing the fresh water spring that runs underneath the property.

Butter and cheese were produced there, and milk was stored in barrels that were kept cold in the rushing waters of the Fox River. The once-tiny creamery grew and later became known as the Geneva Rocks Spring Creamery.

In the late 1890s, the building housed the Lancaster Caramel Company, a subsidiary of the Hershey Chocolate Company. Many of the men who worked at the iron factory across the street would walk down River Lane on their way home after work during this time as the young ladies, who made the candy, would toss caramels out the window to them.

In the years that followed, the creamery building went on to have various uses including the city jail. In 1982 when Geneva began to revive their riverfront district, city officials were looking to redevelop the building that had been vacant for many years. The city approved an ambitious plan for a riverfront hotel by Kent Shodeen of Sho-Deen, Inc., and in 1993, The Herrington opened its doors as the Chicago suburb's top boutique hotel.

The first significant change to the hotel was the restoration of the 3,000-square-foot pump house, which now serves as the hotel's meeting and banquet facility. A twenty-one-room addition, including ultra-luxurious suites overlooking the river below, opened in 2001 and was followed by the opening of the Spa at the Herrington in 2003.

The Herrington continues to stay connected to it history as a creamery. Chocolate chip cookies and milk served in a glass milk bottle are served as part of the hotel's turn-down service and an angelic cow is incorporated into the Herrington Inn & Spa logo

Chapter 7

The Herrington

During the interview process, I had asked the owner why the previous manager had left. What I should have asked was why the previous five managers had left when the hotel had only been open for six years. I quickly realized that I had inherited what many would consider pure chaos, but I was up for the challenge.

The hotel seemed to be run by teenage kids and a few apathetic adults. Within my first month, I had been forced to terminate (or, as I prefer to say, "Employees fire themselves") a significant percentage of the staff for ridiculous and idiotic stunts.

A bellman had left a note in a guest's room that read "Ha-ha, I have your pot, and there is nothing you can do." The soon-to-be-ex bellman was correct that there was not much the guest could do other than complain to me, but the knucklehead was wrong in assuming he was immune to any consequences. The example made to the rest of the staff was even clearer when I found him in the walk-in cooler enjoying his newly acquired stash before being fired and escorted off the property.

I started on November 30 and worked thirty-one consecutive twelve-to-fourteen-hour days in order to keep what seemed like a runaway train from derailing. I was looking forward to watching football at home on the couch on New Year's Day. It was not to be as I received a call at five o'clock in the morning from the night auditor who explained that the nineteen-year-old front desk clerk had called off because of alcohol poisoning, and there was no one else available to cover the shift. My hairline had been receding since my days at the Drake, but I attribute my total baldness to the stress of my first year at the Herrington. In some respects, I was fortunate not to have asked all of the right questions during the interview process. Because if I had, I might not have accepted what would eventually become the perfect opportunity for me to do what I love.

Although the physical building and guest rooms were beautiful, the high turnover and total lack of training had led to mediocre-at-best service. I needed to find several seasoned managers who had the same service expectations that I had . . . and who were capable of developing and implementing standard operating procedures to meet the expectations.

My first target had Four Seasons and Ritz-Carlton experience, and despite compromising ethics, I hired a recruiter to do whatever it took to steal her from a nearby competitor. She made an immediate impact on the front desk, bellmen, and reservations. The recruiter's fee was well worth it, and without my "right arm" at the time, I may have turned out to be the sixth general manager in six years to leave the hotel.

The renovation and transformation of the old city pump house into the hotel's new meeting and banquet space provided me the opportunity to add a new department head. I hired Deanne, an old friend, who had been working for an off-site catering company as the hotel's first director of catering. Although she would have her challenges developing a new staff, systems, and procedures—and not to mention starting from scratch to build up a client base—I think she was happy to not have to lug around chaffing dishes and banquet tables anymore. Deanne remains the longest-tenured department head at the hotel. With over a thousand successful wedding receptions to her credit, along with thousands of other events and meetings, the Herrington's reputation as the area's premier event venue is all thanks to Deanne. Soon she will be planning and executing wedding receptions for daughters of mothers for whom she did the same.

Deanne exudes the qualities of someone who is trying to create guests for life. Her clients become emotionally connected with her, and she treats each event as if it were her own daughter's wedding reception. She has jokingly been invited to join more than one couple on their honeymoon.

Deanne has the ability to ensure that no guest is aware of any behind-the-scenes issues, such as a fire in the kitchen, a red wine stain on a bridal gown, and coaxing shy three-year-old ring bearers to make the trip down the aisle. And with our share of "Bridezillas," we didn't need any additional drama.

The next key acquisition was a chef to lead the culinary team. I was fortunate to entice an executive chef who had worked with me at the Drake Oakbrook Hotel to make his mark at the Herrington. Tom was as comfortable preparing intimate dinner parties for heads of state as being interviewed on television, and he had the creativity to write two books while at the Herrington. Although Tom often had trouble getting his head inside of his toque, he had the culinary skills and charisma to get the hotel established as a significant player in the suburban Chicago culinary world.

Chris, the bellman, started at the Herrington while still in high school and worked as a bellman until he graduated from college. Chris had all the qualities you could ask for in a bellman. You never had to tell Chris a second time to do anything. He enjoyed taking care of guests and was dependable, personable, sincere, and understood that the more guests he came in contact with the more money he would make. Most importantly, Chris had a knack for connecting with guests on a personal level. He had a sense of what each guest needed and did the little things that made a difference and helped separate the Herrington from its competitors.

He was always in the right place at the right time. He would greet guests, open the door, discover their purpose for being there, and made sure the guest knew he was at their disposal. He understood the importance of people coming in to the hotel who had appointments. He assumed they were all VIPs and made them feel as such. Every guest that he encountered who was waiting to meet someone at the hotel was offered a glass of water. That simple gesture got guests off to a great start and set the tone for what could be expected at the Herrington. Chris was also an excellent trainer, evidenced by the good habits that continue with those he trained.

Chapter 8

The Mission

> **Rule 1:**
> *Surround yourself with good people.*

It took time to gain traction, but one by one, we added dedicated team members who helped stabilize and change the culture. Eventually the scales tipped in the right direction and not only did exemplary service start becoming contagious within the team being developed, it started to become the norm. This allowed us to focus more attention on training the weak links and praising those providing a good example, rather than spending time apologizing and repairing damage done by the weak links.

I realized a business plan was needed if we were going to continue raising the level of customer service and began by developing a mission statement.

Some of the key components in my head were:
- Focus on the guest
- Exceed—not just meet—expectations.
- Always be one step ahead.
- Enjoy providing service.

The result was:

"Exceeding our guest's expectations with anticipation and enthusiasm."

I had surrounded myself with the right key players and created a clear mission. The Herrington was finally on the right path to reach its potential.

After being at the Herrington for several months, I wrote a memo titled "Paul's Pet Peeves" with the hope that writing down and sharing the things that drove me nuts would make the remaining lingering issues go away.

For the most part, this method of management effectively modified some behavior, but I felt something wasn't quite right in that it focused entirely on negative behavior—things not to do.

Eventually, I replaced the original memo with a more positive list of examples titled "What makes Paul Happy?"

The goal was to let every new hire know what was expected of them with easy-to-understand examples. Over the years the always-in-flux memo grew to become what is now known as "Ruby's Rules . . . Creating Guests for Life."

Although it was becoming easier and good service was occurring organically, something was still missing. It took me a while to figure it out, but the missing ingredient was **fun**. We incorporated various incentives and contests to create some competitiveness and help break up the monotony. We soon discovered the connection between happy employees and happy guests.

The staff was also beginning to comprehend that if they exceeded the guest's expectations, good things would happen. Some of the changes were small, but still significant, such as when the front office and dining room staffs started asking guests if the purpose of their stay or dining was a special occasion. The staff acknowledged any special events, such as a birthday or anniversary, when guests checked into their room or arrived at the restaurant. In addition, they had a simple card signed by the team waiting on the dining room table or in their guest room. What is significant is the fact that the staff sincerely wanted to make every special occasion memorable, keeping the guests coming back and they enjoyed doing it.

A few months later I received a call from a panicky front desk clerk letting me know that the AAA inspector was in the lobby and wanted to meet with me. I had been through the stressful routine of walking rooms and learning the results of the inspector's anonymous stay while at the Drake.

This meeting started off a little differently after the inspector realized that I was unaware of the previous year's inspection results. He was surprised that I didn't already know that the Herrington did not achieve the required number of points for a four-diamond rating during the last inspection and was on some kind of "secret double probation."

The hotel received an excellent rating for its physical attributes but had technically failed from a service perspective. However, the hotel's rating had not been downgraded based almost entirely on the service provided by Manuel. The inspector encountered this particular employee during multiple key points of the anonymous evaluation. Manuel was the bellman who took him to his room, took the call for the room service order, delivered the room service, and assisted with luggage on the way out.

And although Manuel technically did not meet the AAA four-diamond service requirements, the inspector explained to me that his undeniable sincere desire to please superseded the technical points that he missed. Manuel most definitely had hospitality in his blood, and fortunately, this was clearly apparent to the inspector.

Although we had made it through another year at the four-diamond level, the AAA inspection report was immediately incorporated into a training segment for each area of the hotel. The property has never again been in danger of not meeting the AAA four-diamond requirements and has now received the reward for twenty-five consecutive years.

Chapter 9

Is hospitality in your blood?

Finding team members who are moldable and have "it" is an absolute necessity for success. "It" is when someone is sincerely rewarded by the feeling of knowing that their actions made a positive impact on a guest's experience. Someone can have what appears to be the ideal experience on paper, but not have the sincere desire to please others. Conversely, a candidate may be lacking experience, but clearly demonstrates characteristics needed to create guests for life. The latter will always win in my book. *Great service comes from the heart—not from the head.*

"The quality of your customer service will never exceed the quality of the people providing it."

I often tell hospitality students that it is just as important to realize what you don't want to do as it is to find what you think is your true calling. However, if you don't truly enjoy going out of your way to exceed a guest's expectations, you can cross off almost every position in the hotel business.

"To serve others is to serve one-self."

Properly training all staff before they interact with guests is critical if we want to avoid a compromise in service. But regardless of how much training we provide, it is even more important that staff in high guest contact positions naturally exhibit warmth and hospitality in every guest encounter.

My wife and I were excited to be staying at a five-star hotel rated at the time as the number one business hotel in the world by *Conde Nast* magazine. As we went through the check-in process, the desk clerk clearly completed each of the AAA five-diamond service requirements. However, everything the front desk clerk said came across more like a memorized speech for an architectural boat tour group than a host welcoming a guest . . . Something seemed to be missing. My expectations were high, and they should have been. The desk clerk had failed to make us feel like she was genuinely glad we were there. Instead we felt more like check-in number 43 of 66.

While we can script what our staff members should say, words are often just words. True hospitality requires a sincere desire to serve to accompany the words. This is an emotional characteristic which cannot be taught but is part of a person's DNA, or "in their blood." When hospitality is in your blood, guests appreciate it, your co-workers sense it, and your boss wishes he or she could clone you.

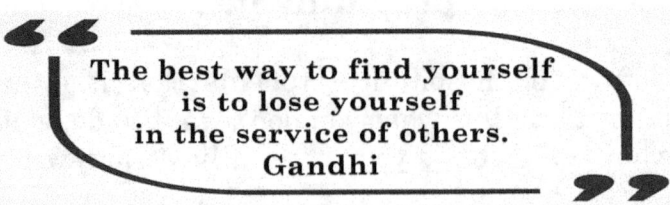

> The best way to find yourself
> is to lose yourself
> in the service of others.
> **Gandhi**

How do we find people with hospitality oozing from their pores? In addition to good benefits and competitive compensation, it helps if your business has a reputation for being a positive place to work.

The hospitality industry is a key entry point into the workforce for many but also offers a variety of career opportunities with varying requirements and responsibilities. No matter the position, finding an employee who fits into the hospitality mold is the first key to sustained success.

And when your business becomes known for promoting from within and/or helping staff members maximize their potential, you greatly increase the odds of attracting the most appropriate people.

One way to get quality candidates to the process is from existing employees. Good people tend to know other people with the traits you appreciate in them. Good employees also exhibit a level of pride and typically want to work with other individuals who are going to make the team stronger.

> **Rule 4:**
> *Treat those you are serving in the manner in which you would like to be treated.*

Critical customer service skills, which we should be looking for and expecting when hiring, begin with empathy. In order to keep our customers happy, we need to understand their expectations and how they feel. To do that, we must step into the customer's shoes. If a guest has saved for months in order to be able to splurge on a special weekend, we need to perceive how important it might be for little things to go right through the eyes of the guest. We need to communicate, focus, and treat the guest the way we want to be communicated to, focused on, and treated. The golden rule applies here.

We need to find staff members who exude positivity. They need to smile, show eagerness to please, are willing to assist wherever needed, and outwardly show they are glad to be where they are.

Staff members who interact with guests need to have or develop patience. Nobody likes waiting in line to check in or to wait for their room service order that was promised to arrive fifteen minutes earlier. While we can't expect our guests to be patient, having a sense of calmness can help diffuse problems and allows us to focus on the guest's needs.

Other important qualities include politeness, friendliness, sincerity, attentiveness, and timeliness. Most of these characteristics don't require any special training. It is either part of their persona or it isn't. The key is asking the right questions during the interview that provide a clue as to whether the candidate has the characteristics we are searching for—or is moldable enough to develop the necessary traits.

> **Rule 5:**
> *Don't let training be an excuse for compromised service.*

Training is much more than having new team members shadow another team member. Getting new staff off to a good start is vital and a proper orientation is part of the process. It also helps to have clearly defined job descriptions for each position. We need to set up our staff for success and never put new staff out on the floor or in situations to interact with guests until they are ready.

If you are having dinner at a restaurant and your server has a nametag that has "In Training" printed on it, does that mean you should expect and accept inferior service?

Does giving advance notice that someone may not be ready to be on their own make compromised service okay? Will your bill be discounted in proportion to the quality of the service you receive? If a staff member has not received enough training to be able to provide the level of service our guests expect, then they should not be on their own or put in a situation where they are set up to fail.

When a supervisor takes the time to ensure new employees get off to a good start, it is a sign that they truly care and want the entire team to succeed. Training never stops, and we must have the goal of continuously improving. To achieve this, we need motivation and measurement. In a perfect world, all staff members are self-motivated and possess an innate desire to serve others. However, we cannot afford to assume this and must also provide gratitude and positive reinforcement for a job well done.

It should be exciting and rewarding for a supervisor to print off a copy of a review or comment card mentioning a staff member by name who made a positive impression on a guest and post it on the employee bulletin board. Emotional rewards should come from your team's success, not yours.

In regards to measuring improvement of our service levels, if we can strive to improve just one percent every day, use one percent more positivity in our emails, respond one percent faster to a guest request or to return a call; if we try to improve our customer satisfaction score by a single percentage point, the compounding impact over time is amazing.

We must also solicit feedback from our staff. However, we can receive oodles of feedback from our staff and the worst thing we can do is to agree with what they say and do nothing. When staff feel that there is no point to bring up problems to their supervisor because it is unlikely that anything will be done to fix the problem, or worse yet, that by bringing up a problem, it will come back to bite them, you can guarantee you have a morale problem—or it is on its way. Always take employee feedback seriously and respond in a timely manner.

Retaining outstanding team members for as long as possible, and having a favorable "farm system" for replacing those who do leave, is critical to reducing the peaks and valleys and maintaining a consistently high level of service. Retention requires a positive and rewarding work environment.

What keeps outstanding employees content? Respect, fairness, a decent meal, and consistent hours are obvious factors which help to create a happy work force. It also requires giving the staff the necessary tools to succeed.

> **"Train your staff well enough that they are prepared to leave and treat them well enough that they want to stay."**

We must always provide clear expectations to the team. This begins even before they are hired. Goals and objectives should be consistent, documented, and attainable. A detailed job description, orientation, and a comprehensive employee handbook are all vital tools needed to get staff off to a good start.

If you hire and retain excellent people, you keep guests happy. If you keep guests happy, they return, tell others, and help sustain business. The concept is no different than in any other service industry. I would hate to guess the percentage of room attendants who actually look forward to going to work to clean up other people's garbage, but if you can keep them motivated and positive, good things trickle up.

> **Rule 7:**
> *All team members must be empowered to make decisions.*

While the satisfaction and long-term retention of your employees should always be on the radar, the greater goal is to build a high-performing team that adds value to the guest's experience, from check-in to check-out.

Assuming we are hiring line employees with a reasonable amount of common sense, we need to give our team the approval to make decisions on the spot in order to retain a guest. This means we need to allow our team members to make mistakes. These mistakes, however, can and must be utilized as training opportunities so we can offer more appropriate solutions and avoid repeating them.

In the "old days" of the hospitality industry, regardless of whether you stayed in an expensive, five-star resort or a budget chain, customers knew pretty much what to expect. Now, with anti-service options such as Airbnb and trendy boutique chains on the scene, great service has never mattered more to hotel consumers. And when you consider the impact of online reviews for the world to see, a hotel's reputation can appear fragile. This makes creating guests for life absolutely critical to success and the importance of your focus on customer service.

Chapter 10

First and Last Impressions

> *Rule 8:*
> *Do it right the first time.*

Surely the brain trust behind the world's largest company has greeters at their entrances for another reason besides making sure you go in and out the correct door. The feeling of being welcomed is vital, whether it's to someone's home, a hotel, or a big department store.

Getting off to a good start doesn't just apply to the bellmen or the front desk. It means every staff member has the opportunity to set or impact the tone for the remainder of the guest's stay.

When a guest gets off to a bad start, they have a way of noticing the M&M left by the previous guest behind the dresser, or that the room service waiter was wearing two different socks. However, when a guest gets off to a good start, small problems usually remain small problems and are often overlooked. When something goes wrong at the beginning of a stay, a trigger is set for the very same guest to write a letter listing problems that they are forced to look for or invent.

An employee could defend themselves by stating they were just being frugal when warming up a stale pot of coffee instead of brewing a fresh pot to serve to a guest. In reality, the guest was left with a bitter taste in his mouth and may never be back. Do it right the first time so you don't have to spend the time and energy to do it right later.

I have learned a thing or two about manners from my father in-law, Cecil Baird. For seventy years, Cecil carried two clean and pressed white handkerchiefs . . . one for himself inside his suit pocket and one if a lady should need it. This habit has rubbed off on me. For those who might find this sexist or old fashioned, you only have to experience once the gratitude from a teary-eyed mother of a bride who just received a timely hanky to appreciate the importance of old school manners.

It seems like politeness in our society peaked in the early sixties during the days of Miss Manners and *Leave it to Beaver*. Never assume that new staff members understand the basic principles of etiquette and good manners. Opening the car door for a lady, waiting for people to exit the elevator before entering, and sometimes even saying "please" and "thank you" often need to be trained with the millennial generation. But don't fall into the trap and think for a minute that basic etiquette and good manners are not expected—or that providing them is anything special.

The bar must be raised much higher to achieve great service. However, it is scary to me how often guests are surprised and feel special because their chair was pulled out for them before sitting in the dining room, or even hearing "please" and "thank you" from a drive-through worker at the local fast food restaurant.

Chick-fil-A has the highest revenue per store of any of the major fast food chains, and much of their success is attributed to having well-trained staff. And it all starts with their requirement to use "please" and "thank you" in every appropriate situation.

The way we look, what we say, and how we say it . . .

Do we portray a sense of focused urgency when approaching a guest to provide service? Are you dressed in a manner and wearing a name tag to make it obvious you are an employee of the hotel? Or, do you give the guest a warm and cheerful greeting to make it clear you are glad they are here and you are at their service? Were you polite? Did you show good manners? Did you use good grammar? Did you speak too loudly . . . too softly . . . too quickly? What was your body language like? Were your shoes polished, and did they match your belt? Do you have the remnants of your smoke break on your breath? Is your hair combed, and are you clean shaven? Were you sitting down, chewing gum and looking at anything other than the eyes of the person you were supposed to be serving?

Typically, the most critical point of contact in a hotel happens at the front desk. When checking in, guests want to be looked at, talked to, and smiled at. They want us to pick up on their emotional signals, listen to them, and to be of further assistance. And most importantly, they want us to thank them for choosing our hotel.

Sometimes our best opportunity to make an impression on a guest is during our last encounter. It is vital that when guests are departing that you greet them, ask them about their experience, and thank them. We must be sincere in the way we show appreciation for their patronage. If the guest points out something not quite right at any point during their stay, we need to make sure they know we are going to react and document it appropriately. And if a staff member is mentioned because he or she did something commendable, the guest should be assured that the employee will be properly recognized.

Chapter 11

Conflict Resolution

> **Rule 10:**
> When "no means no," and when it means an opportunity lost.

The word "No" is a word that should rarely be heard in any hospitality setting. "No" should be the reply only to requests that are illegal, immoral, unethical, or not in the best interest of the business. Taking the time to suggest alternatives, rather than simply saying, "No, we don't do that," is part of extending hospitality.

"I don't know" falls in the same category. "Let me find the answer to that for you," or "Let me put you in touch with . . . who will know the answer," are always better responses.

I once overheard a guest with young children ask a front desk clerk if there were any amusement parks nearby. The simple answer and truth was "no," as the nearest amusement park was an hour and a half away, but the reply was, "No, but we do have a minor league baseball team, and they have a home game tonight. Would you like me to look into getting tickets?" The family had so much fun at the game that they have become guests and Kane County Cougars fans for life. The front desk clerk was able to tell the guest about an activity they didn't even know existed but was perfect for that family.

An older couple walked up to the host at three in the afternoon and asked to see a menu because they were interested in having lunch. The host politely replied that the restaurant was currently closed, but they could sit at a table in the lobby where an "all day" menu was available. The couple peered into the dining room and asked if they could be seated in the empty room. They also asked if they could order from a lunch menu. The host explained that they were in-between meal periods, that the all-day menu included some lunch items but they would need to be seated in the lobby.

Although the host was technically accurate with his responses, his train of thought was clearly not on target with the hotel's mission statement. Instead of figuring out a way to accommodate the guest's requests, the host defaulted to the easy way out.

Was there any reason that the guests could not be seated in the dining room? Was there any reason that their menu options were limited? On this particular occasion, the answer to both questions was no.

The bartender had nothing to do and would have been happy to have the customers. The dining room was set for dinner, but with a couple of adjustments, a table could have easily been made ready. A trip to the kitchen to confirm that there was nothing on the lunch menu that could not be made might have been a good thing to do, but the response to the couple's request to be offered the lunch menu should have been, "Let me confirm with the kitchen that there is nothing they cannot make," rather than restricting their options.

Unfortunately, the couple walked out of the hotel disappointed and still hungry. The bottom line is: while there are times when we must follow guidelines such as hours that the dining room is open, and when certain menus are available, our first thought must always be to figure out how we can exceed our guest's expectations even if we have to veer from posted "guidelines." With few exceptions, employees will never be in trouble for breaking or "bending" rules in order to provide gratifying service.

Sometimes we do need to say no in order to be consistent from one guest to the next, or to avoid chaos when policies become completely obsolete. But again, giving the guest options of what you *can* do is always better than telling them what you *can't* do.

There are times when the needs, or wants, of guests conflict with the best interests of the hotel. Guests who tip well and have a need to be acknowledged beyond the point of being pampered, can sometimes commandeer personnel resources to the point that letting the guest know you are unable to meet their expectations is the right thing to do.

A little greed in a bellman can be a positive quality when it relates to being in the right place at the right time, hustling, or going out of their way to provide service. However, once an employee lets the anticipation of a big tip influence their actions, it can be a hard habit to break for both the staff member and the guest.

A frequent guest was known for making it worth staff members' time and effort for taking care of his last-minute, time-consuming requests. It was not always in the best interests of the hotel, however, to carry out his requests. The night before the latest cell phone version was to be released, Mr. "Unreasonable Request" told a bellman he wanted him to be waiting in line at the Apple store the next morning prior to opening, to purchase a phone for his daughter. If we have enough notice, are covering our costs, and not compromising other guests' experiences, there are few guest requests we shouldn't try to fulfill.

However, the scenario above would have entailed three hours of overtime with no bellman on site to assist guests on a busy check-out morning. It is also important that we don't continue to "feed the monster," or provide an all-encompassing rational for employees to make the wrong decisions. Once we allow the staff to universally justify their actions because "I was just trying to meet the guest's expectations so I could create a guest for life," it becomes difficult to maintain a balance between empowering our staff to provide outstanding service, and knowing when limits need to be set. Unfortunately, despite several attempts of compromising with the guest, we were forced to let him know that we could no longer accommodate him at the Herrington.

Although dogs have always been allowed at the Herrington, there was an incident that caused a revocation of the pet-friendly policy. When two giant Irish Wolfhounds broke through the patio screen of their room, ran amuck all over the courtyard, darted into a different guest's room through their open screen door, and then into the hotel lobby where they cleaned off the plates of two guests having dessert by the fireplace, you would have thought by the screams of horror that the giant dogs were rabid and attacking everyone in sight. No one ended up bitten or trampled, but the repercussions from what came to be known as "the wolfhound incident," was so bad that I rescinded the dog policy for the next year. During the dog moratorium, instead of saying "Sorry, we don't allow dogs," the staff were instructed to say, "No, but we have two local kennels that we work with."

Rule 11: Adversity creates opportunity.

Encountering a guest who is frustrated, disappointed, or even angry can often be the best situation to make a lasting impression. Unless the guest's expectations are completely unreasonable, or their intentions are deceitful, we need to always consider these challenges as opportunities. We are now in a situation to show the guest how important they are to us and that our goal is to make things right and retain them as a valued patron. Providing the best possible service is often not the easiest thing to do, but it is always the right thing to do. The most challenging situations can sometimes create the most clear-cut path to creating guests for life.

It should always be easy to make a decision based on the mindset, "What is going to make the guest happy or exceed their expectations?" Hard decisions usually involve situations where we have already disappointed a guest and are scrambling to make things right.

Regardless of whether you are in the midst of "walking" a few hundred guests or a simple room change, empathy is a necessity even if it takes a little bit of robotic numbness to get you through the day.

Do you genuinely think a guest cares how the hotel got overbooked, or why they were accidentally checked into the wrong room, or even why their toilet overflowed? Not really . . . sometimes all it takes is a sincere apology and acknowledgment, and other times, it takes allowing the guest to vent and then crafting an answer to the dreaded, "What are you going to do to make things right?" question.

The basic principles of service are simple if you consistently treat guests the way we would like to be treated. The hard part is realizing that problems may not be our fault, they might not be anybody's fault, or they could even be the guest's fault, but it just doesn't matter. We need to learn to treat each guest individually and strive to never lose our compassion for wanting to serve others.

Special occasion destinations like the Herrington are often filled with guests with high expectations. If a guest's experience has been compromised for any reason; such as a thunderstorm that didn't allow the guest to enjoy their balcony, or a guest didn't receive turndown service because they left their do not disturb sign on the door, we still need to show empathy and let the guest know we are truly sorry their experience was compromised. And if the problem is your fault, or due to something that was within the hotel's control, we need to not only be empathetic, apologetic, and take responsibility, we need to make things right.

A couple came into the dining room disappointed after not being able to get a table at a nearby restaurant. As the guests were waiting to be seated, the restaurant manager overheard the wife complaining to her husband about not getting her favorite minestrone soup at the other restaurant. The manager sent the bellman to the other restaurant for a to-go container of minestrone soup, which was then presented to the wife during dinner. This couple was so overwhelmed with the thoughtfulness that they are now guests for life and return for every special occasion dinner.

Other times you can make a difference by going the extra mile. A coughing, sick guest once checked into the hotel and mentioned how much work she had left to do despite wishing she could just go to bed. The front desk clerk took initiative and sent the bellman to purchase throat lozenges, who took them to the sick guest along with some hot tea and honey. The guest did not request assistance, but she is now a guest for life.

> **Rule 12:**
> **The guest is not always right, but they are still our guest and need to stay that way.**

Staff members are empowered to use their discretion to do whatever it takes to retain a customer. Offer solutions to problems in a non-condescending manner and be sincere about your lone goal of retention. Guests may exaggerate, lie, not have all the information regarding a situation, or not realize that certain problems are beyond our control, but we must always do whatever it takes to attempt to have the guest leave with the feeling that we did whatever we could to resolve a problem.

Regardless of whether or not a problem is directly related to your own or someone else's negligence or carelessness, we cannot afford to get defensive, make excuses, or take things personally.

Sometimes all it takes is a sincere apology and acknowledgement that you will make the appropriate manager aware of the issue. Sometimes it just means making a decision on the spot. A wrong decision is often better than no decision at all, which may leave the guest with the feeling that no one cares or is capable of correcting a problem.

A guest booked a weekend spa package months in advance as a birthday present for his wife. Although it was recommended that he reserve his wife's massage as soon as possible because they fill up fast, the husband procrastinated until the week before their arrival to call the spa. All the treatment rooms were booked for the day and the only option, according to the spa employee, was to reschedule for another date.

Despite realizing he should have called sooner, the domino effect of problems he now faced brought him to a combination of tears and anger. He had arranged for his in-laws from out of town to babysit their three children for the weekend, he had been working as much overtime as he could to save money, and he had juggled his schedule to have the weekend off. The thought of how disappointed his wife would be was unimaginable. Despite his desperate pleas to the spa employee to attempt to accommodate his wife, he was again told, "The treatment rooms are all fully committed, and there is nothing that we can do."

Although building another treatment room was not an option, why was an in-room massage not offered? The problem was not that there wasn't a massage therapist available; the issue was the treatment rooms were booked. The real problem in this situation was the employee did the easy thing but not the right thing to come up with options of what could be done.

> **Rule 13:**
> *Patience is more than a virtue. It's also a customer service necessity.*

It is a simple fact that some customers get angry. Some customers require extra attention and sensitivity for us to effectively communicate with them. The worst thing you, or anyone on your team, can do is lose your cool.

Even if the guest across the counter from us has just berated us for something we didn't do, we must remain calm, cool, and collected and do our best to put the guest at ease. Reacting to a guest's anger with an agitated approach typically leads to an escalation of the problem. Offer sympathy to get to the root of the cause and take the required action. It's imperative to avoid taking each complaint on a personal level. A customer has every right to be displeased if the hotel service is not satisfactory. One of the biggest challenges is to realize the complaint is typically about the service someone else provided, or didn't provide, and not about the person dealing with the irate guest at the moment.

Be a good listener. Sometimes a guest just wants to be heard. It is important to have all the facts before you determine a solution, but be sure to respond in a timely manner, and don't wait until a guest has left the property to resolve the issue.

Respond with an apology and pay attention to what your guest has to say. An apology will calm down an agitated guest, and you'll be able to address the problem once you understand the issue. Using sentences such as, "I understand you have every right to feel angry..." or "I will let my supervisor know about this issue immediately..." will provide reassurance to irate hotel guests. Avoid transferring the call if the complaint is via the telephone. There's nothing worse than getting transferred to a voicemail box other than being inadvertently disconnected.

Always go the extra mile and request that the guest place their next hotel room request through you so that all requirements will be taken care of personally. This is one of the easiest ways to win back the trust of an irate hotel guest.

> **Rule 14:**
> To be or not to be...Be assuring, sincere, and eager to please. Don't be unsure, presumptuous, or untimely.

We need to avoid becoming defensive and never be tempted to make something up to get out of a jam. Passing the buck and making light of a guest's concerns doesn't solve any problems either.

Instead, we need to acknowledge the problem, accept accountability, take measures to reduce the chances of the problem reoccurring, and make things right. This requires empathy, follow-up, and documentation.

Solicit feedback from check-in through check-out. One of the most important things about guest satisfaction is keeping ahead of any negative influences on our guest's experience. The sooner we know that the guest has a problem or concern, the more likely we will be able to make things right. Waiting for a guest to post a bad review is not ideal. And then there are the guests who may not take the time to fill out a comment card or write a review . . . they just simply will never come back.

Questions such as, "Are you comfortable? How is your stay? Is there anything you require? Did you enjoy the food?" will help gain quick feedback.

Keeping track of our guest's likes and dislikes is a basic standard. If a guest has a problem with their room, document what happened in their profile. If the guest comes back and gives us an opportunity to redeem ourselves, the least we can do is make the extra effort to ensure their next stay is perfect.

For example, if the guest didn't get a good night's sleep because of noise from the lobby, on their next stay don't select a room near the lobby. It seems too simple, but if we don't take the time to input, we are destined to repeat our mistakes.

We must strive to win back our customers one at a time, and try as we might, we need to accept the fact that it is unlikely we will get them all back.

> **Rule 15:**
> *Sometimes you need to accept the fact that you can't make everyone happy and there are some guests who are better off being someone else's problem.*

Guest complaints sometimes appear bogus. Every now and then we find ourselves dealing with a complaining guest who appears, at least on the surface, to be making bonus claims in an attempt to get something for nothing. I can't tell you how tempting it is to call them out, to let them know you are on to their deceit, and not only will you not be comping their room but you've added them to the blacklist and will never be allowed in the hotel again.

> **Rule 16:**
> *Solicit guest feedback and respond when you get it.*

The customer's always right, right? The ability to swallow one's pride and accept blame or negative feedback is crucial. I was close to certain that a guest attempted to flush something that had no business being in the toilet so that their room would flood, and we would comp their stay. To make things worse, they waited until a day after they checked out to send an email demanding a refund, and they were angry that they felt forced to contact me to resolve the problem instead of me initiating the resolution.

I had a detailed account of what happened from maintenance and the staff member who cleaned up the mess. They both explained that the toilet had actually backed up twice during this guest's stay, and that it had been clearly explained after the first snaking that sanitary napkins should not be flushed. I had also received a report from the manager on duty who stated he noticed that there was a note in the guest's history about their previous stay being comped due to a toilet overflow.

Well, fool me once shame on you, but fool me twice shame on me. I replied by email to the guest and basically told them that they were fortunate that we didn't charge them for the guest room below them where the couple on their wedding night was woken by toilet water dripping on them through the ceiling from the room above. And I certainly wasn't going to comp their stay for something "self-inflicted." In hindsight, a second after I clicked the send key, I knew there was little to gain by further infuriating a guest, even if they were asking for something they didn't deserve.

However, I went from feeling good about putting con artists in their place, to reservations about how I responded, to sheer embarrassment when I eventually became aware of both sides of the story and the truth. Although sanitary napkins were snaked out of the toilet twice during the guest's stay, when I found out they were actually the victim of water coming down the ceiling from the toilet above during their previous stay, and the wife was in her late sixties and unlikely in need of sanitary napkins, all I could do was put my tail between my legs, apologize, and attempt to make things right.

In the hospitality business, we are trained to do whatever it takes to make things right for our guests. Although empathy and sincerity are the first two traits needed in successfully resolving guest issues, having confidence, common sense, and understanding that sometimes no matter what hoops you jump through it isn't going to be enough to win back some guests.

There was the couple who came to the Herrington to celebrate their tenth wedding anniversary. They brought everything imaginable to make the night more romantic, including about a dozen candles and some kind of scented oil that should be banned from any establishment that has fabric or carpet. Not only did the couple manage to start a bathrobe on fire, spill wax all over the carpet, ruin a comforter and carpet, set off the fire alarm and force the evacuation of the entire hotel, they had the gall to insist that we comp their stay because their special occasion was ruined. The couple made a scene at the front desk in front of a lobby full of guests and threatened to post a bad review on the internet if we didn't comply.

Sometimes you just have to accept the fact that attempting to retain some guests is a lost cause and that complying with every demand is often not in the best interest of the hotel. Although it is always disappointing when you lose a patron, there was some satisfaction when I was able to have the bogus review removed from an internet site and we won the credit card dispute for their bill, which included the room charge and replacement of a comforter and a charred bathrobe.

We may not have control over a guest's attitude, but we must always have the belief that every one of us has the ability to influence a guest's experience. Occasions when we give up trying to make sure the guest leaves with a positive impression should be few and far between.

I had no interest in retaining the patronage of an intoxicated, belligerent guest who trashed his room, promised to have me fired, and then managed to land a juicy hocker on my suit jacket while I was in the process of evicting him. Fortunately, the positive experiences far outweigh the negative ones. Unfortunately, spitting guests are tough to forget.

Chapter 12

Preparing for Success

> **Rule 17:**
> *Anticipate, follow-up, and be proactive.*

Offer assistance before a guest asks for help. If you just finished delivering a room service order to a room, the tray will eventually need to be removed. It is unlikely that the guest would not appreciate a call an hour or so later asking the guest if they are ready to have their tray removed.

If you have ever been on a cruise ship with kids, you have probably had a rabbit, or some other cute animal made out of wash cloths waiting in your room. The first time had a little wow factor for you and a lot from the kids The second time it made little impact on you, but the kids still got a kick out of it. What would happen if the steward did not do the towel origami at all? All the little things add up, and although we don't know for sure if a guest will appreciate when the room attendant folds the corners of the toilet paper or the server refolds a napkin when a guest leaves the table to use the restroom, not doing them because you think the guest does not care is a compromise to good service.

One of our largest clients, who provided diversity training to executives, held a four-day meeting in early November with attendees from all over the country. Many within the group came from California and Texas. Unfortunately, no one in the group must have checked the weather forecast and/or packed appropriately. With outdoor team-building activities planned, temperatures in the upper thirties and no one with a coat, the facilitator would have cancelled the outdoor plans if he would have been at any other property than the Herrington. Before the client even realized that there might be a problem with a lack of appropriate clothing for the group, the banquet captain had already assembled enough hats, gloves, and jackets to outfit everyone. Everything continued as planned, attendees stayed warm, and the bond with the client became even stronger. Although this situation seemed routine and the staff's reaction was innate, the guests who were provided what they considered VIP treatment surely retold the story of how the Herrington staff went above and beyond the call of duty.

I am often asked, "What is the craziest guest request you have ever had?"

At some point I stopped telling about the celebrity requests like having a chili cheese hot dog waiting on the tarmac for one of them, or the list of pre-arrival requests Steve Martin had . . . for his dog.

I realized that truly amazing service isn't about fulfilling a famous person's lists of demands, but rather the extraordinary things that staff members have done for ordinary people without being asked. Such as when staff members do things like brushing the snow from a guest's car without being asked or expecting anything in return.

"Hear without being told; see without being shown; and know without being asked."

Rule 18: Focus on what we can control.

We need to focus our attention on things we can influence or situations where we can make a difference—and not waste energy on things that are beyond our control. We can't make the impending storm clouds disappear for the distraught bride hoping to be married outside, but we can be reassuring and make it clear that we have a contingency plan for every possible scenario.

Traveling with my family, I pulled into a resort in central Indiana knowing in advance that the property was in the final stages of an extensive renovation. I entered the lobby and approached the front desk where the clerk was busy on a phone call, which I quickly learned had something to do with a recently delivered order of laminated flooring that was the wrong color. The clerk, who I found out later was actually the front office manager, never lifted his head to acknowledge me and continued to argue with the person on the other end of the phone about when the mistake was going to be rectified.

I was becoming impatient and was tempted to find alternate lodging, but the gentleman finally finished his phone call and said, "Can I help you?" as if I had no business interrupting his very important phone call. If I were to honestly answer his question, I would have responded, "Yes, I would like to be warmly greeted and made to feel welcome." However, I held back and against my better judgment registered into the resort.

The entire experience was anti-hospitality. We were clearly an inconvenience to the staff, as the property was open but not prepared to receive guests. The physical structure was usable and capable of generating revenue, but the staff was clearly not trained and clueless as to how to provide any kind of service.

The restaurant employee who handed us our check after we went through the buffet line adhered to the "Please seat yourself" sign and didn't even get up off her bar stool when we entered. Her shirt was untucked, her hair was dirty, and she seemed perturbed that we interrupted her viewing of what must have been an important episode of *Judge Judy*. I sent a letter to the general manager offering some specific constructive criticism. His response was consistent with the service I received from the staff at the resort . . . there was none.

"The Bellman Spiel"

I'm sure every new bellman at the Herrington is warned to expect "the bellman spiel" from Mr. Ruby. I have made it my personal mission to be involved in the training of the employee who is often the first person who has an opportunity to make an impression on guests. Although I don't think I come across as intimidating, when new bellmen are hired, they are told to see me in my office to get "the spiel."

I typically hear a nervous knock on my door, have the bellman come in, and take a seat. I attempt to put them at ease from the beginning by telling stories of my first job at

McDonald's, and how I wish I could have worked at a place like the Herrington. My goal is to help the young men get off to a good start by clearly defining what is expected of them and teach them some tricks on how they can increase their tips, but most importantly, how they can impact a guest's stay.

I use this example: imagine a guest who has spent the past six hours getting from New York to Chicago with delays and bad weather. The guest has rented a car and has just arrived at the Herrington parking lot. He opens his trunk to remove his luggage, wheels his suitcase across the street and down the stairs, opens the huge front doors, struggles down the stone steps in the lobby, and finally gets checked at the front desk. All of a sudden, a bellman comes out from behind the front desk and asks if the gentleman would like help with his luggage. I ask the new hire, "What do you think the odds are that the guest will take him up on the offer?" The typical response is "Not good."

Next, I tell the young man sitting across from me, who is nodding his head in an effort to acknowledge his understanding, to imagine that the bellman intercepts the guest before he opens the front door. "What are the odds then?

And what if the bellman is there to assist before the guest exits his car, has the door open for him, and is ready to pull the suitcase out of the trunk?"

I explain that if he is not in a position to provide service, regardless of whether the service is expected by the guest or not, you lose an opportunity to make a positive impact on a guest's stay, and you have lost an opportunity to receive a tip.

Rule 19:
See and experience what guests see and experience.

Considering the guest's perspective is the only one that matters. We need to put ourselves through the same flow chart that a guest goes through. The process begins at the very first point of contact. This could be the website, on the phone, or someone walking into the hotel without a reservation. We must periodically look at our website as if we are the consumer, call and make a reservation, and walk in the front door. We must notice and remove the posting on our website for a wine dinner that happened three months ago, hear the reservationist use the guest's name, and see and pick up the cigarette butt in the parking lot. We must also sit in every seat in the building and lay in every bed. It's amazing what we can walk by day after day and not notice, but being where a guest would be, we magically see the debris on the patio, the smudge on the window, or maybe the cobweb that you can only see when you sit in a specific chair at a specific time of day when the sun shines at just the right angle.

We also need to go through the same routines and processes as our guests to see, hear, and feel what our guests experience.

In regards to training, managers need to not only teach the proper procedures and policies, but also periodically test the staff to make sure they continue to do what they were taught.

The use of "secret shoppers," or anonymous inspectors, can provide positive reinforcement when things are running smoothly, and conversely, can show weak links and areas in need of improvement. I periodically have shoppers stay at the hotel to hopefully confirm that service levels are being met and service standards are being followed. I supply the shopper with a simple list of yes or no questions, which help to objectively determine if employees are compliant with performing specific tasks or procedures. I also encourage shoppers to identify individual staff members who make a positive or negative impact on how they feel about the hotel.

A recent shopper's report confirmed that the turndown attendant was flawless and completed every task on the list. However, the report also revealed that the bellman who escorted the shoppers up to their room knew nothing about the spa, area restaurants, or if the hotel had a health club. To make things worse, the bellman's response was simply, "I don't know," and did not follow up with answers. Without this inspection, who knows how many guests would have received compromised service before anyone realized, or how long it would take to acknowledge the turndown attendant for a job well done?

Lights, music, and atmosphere (LMA) are a good basis for making sure things are in place in preparation of receiving guests, but what else can be added?

How about C for cleanliness and P for perspective? Anything within the guest's sight lines should be clean, organized and at proper lighting and music volume levels. I have employees sit at every seat in the dining room and look in every direction to see what a guest sees.

One of my pet peeves is to walk in the lobby in the morning to find the shades still drawn and the music too low or off. It always seems crazy to me that employees don't notice the LMA. This is why we sometimes need checklists for staff to follow to minimize the little things that have a tendency to slip through the cracks and have the potential to add up.

Rule 20: Create a memorable experience.

Is a nice clean room with a view, or a well-prepared steak served by a professional server, enough? This may be enough to get a guest to return, and it might be enough for a guest to post a positive review on the internet. Should we be satisfied with "satisfied" guests? Not if we want to achieve our mission of exceeding our guest's expectations. And not if we intend on providing the type of experience that creates a guest for life.

A memorable experience requires providing everything a guest was expecting, plus as many unexpected "treats" as possible. A treat might be as simple as a card signed by the staff congratulating a couple celebrating an anniversary in the dining room, or as complex as arranging to have the mascot of the local single A baseball team make an appearance for an 80th birthday celebration.

Guest retention takes more than service: it takes providing hospitality. We are in the service industry, so providing high-quality service means you are just doing your job. Our guests expect more.

To a certain extent, hotels are a commodity—at least to guests. Most unhappy guests won't even bother to give you a bad review, they'll just book elsewhere next time they're in town. Offering a clean comfortable room at competitive rates . . . so what? We need to make our property stand out. What is our differentiator? We usually can't change the view from the balcony or increase the size of a room. The one thing we can change is the service we provide our guests.

Service is our perspective—what we do. Experience is the guest's perspective—what they receive.

Rule 21: Know how to make a guest feel special.

Value each guest as if they are not only a VIP guest, but the hotel's only guest, at least at the moment. Embrace their unique preferences, interests, and expectations.

Know who your guests are and why they are staying with you. Ask during the time of making a reservation, "Are you celebrating a special occasion?" Value, quality, and good customer service can mean different things to different guests.

Frequent travelers want their accommodations to feel like a home away from home, but with an upgrade. One of the problems with travel is you can't always do for yourself as you can at home. You may not be able to fix your usual evening snack like at home, or tighten a loose screw on a lamp, which can cause frustration. Being responsive in reacting to guest requests helps reduce the opportunity for frustration.

Rule 22: Keep thorough records.

If Mr. Jones requests an extra pillow or towels on his visit, don't just provide them on request. Keep track and make sure they are waiting in his room before he arrives on his next stay. Don't just place them there without remarking; when he checks in, say, "Mr. Jones, we know you like extra towels, so you'll find them waiting for you in your room."

Hosting VIPs and celebs can be exciting for the staff of the hotel and add an exciting energy to the atmosphere. Often, it is these stays when you may see the best in yourself and your staff members in terms of service and attention. The bigger the guest, the harder we try. It is human nature to want to treat those we view as special in an exceptional way. These stays can provide something much more important; they can help you design a vision of exactly how every guest should be treated.

Garrett Richter, president and CEO of First National Bank of Florida said, "If we roll out the red carpet for billionaires, they won't even notice it. If we roll it out for millionaires, they expect it. If we roll out the red carpet for thousandaires, they appreciate it. And if we roll out the red carpet for hundredaires, they tell everybody they know."

Capture the name at the time of reservation and use it at every opportunity. Anyone going to or calling a guest's room should know and use their name.

Why is calling a guest by name important? My response to employees asking this question is to compare how you feel after a bellman or the cashier at the grocery store says, "Thank you, Mr. Jones," compared to just "thank you." It depends on the situation, but hopefully the guest feels special with the more personal touch of using their name. This is even truer if it is a repeat guest. If housekeeping or a bellman were delivering a toothbrush to a room, I can't think of any excuse why an employee would not greet a guest by name when the guest answers the door.

"Remember that a person's name is, to him/her, the sweetest and most important sound in any language." Dale Carnegie

Rule 23: When is it okay to assume?

You never know if the person asking for a tour is a meeting planner anonymously checking out the property for a convention, or a recently engaged bride searching for a reception venue. You also never know who is an AAA inspector or restaurant critic, so assume everyone who walks in the door is a VIP and treat him or her as such. You can also assume that if you put forth the effort to make a positive impact on every guest you encounter, you have a better chance of achieving our mission statement:

"Exceeding our guests' expectations with anticipation and enthusiasm."

Giving good customer service means being sincere, listening, following up, and communicating well with guests as well as other employees and managers.

It is okay to assume that every guest checking into the hotel is either the AAA inspector or a meeting planner coming to do a surprise site inspection, but never predetermine that anyone is not deserving of anything less than excellent service.

Assuming that each and every guest may have an impact on your paycheck is okay. Even more importantly, we should assume that we can make a positive impact on every guest's experience. This means making sure the weakest link is trained, at the very least, to always put the guest first. Employees at every level must be empowered to do whatever it takes to take care of our guests as long as they don't do anything unethical or jeopardize the hotel financially.

> **Rule 24:**
> **Never leave a guest to do something for themselves that you can do for them.**

When a guest asks for a restaurant recommendation, don't just hand them our three-ring binder of menus. Solicit more information on the type of restaurant they are looking for, suggest options based on their response, offer to make a reservation for them, and if possible, follow up and ask how they enjoyed the restaurant. Go one step further and offer them a ride to and from the restaurant.

If you are in the hallway and meet a guest who asks where the ice machine is, ask for their room number, request the ice bucket and let them know you will bring ice to their room rather than simply directing them to the ice machine.

Always escort, never point. Whenever feasible, personally escort the guest to the elevator, the rest room, the dining room, etc.

My wife and I were invited to a special dinner with Michael J. Fox in New York City. We made plans for a long weekend and scheduled an early flight on the morning of our dinner. We arrived at the airport and checked our luggage. The agent informed us that our flight had been delayed due to bad weather on the east coast. We weren't too concerned as we had plenty of time, but when our flight was actually canceled, we started to panic.

After several hours in the airport, and running out of options that would get us to New York in time to make the dinner, we finally found a flight to Newark that "on paper" would logistically work, but left us no margin for error. Our sense of relief turned into disappointment when we realized that we would not be able to retrieve our luggage in time to catch our new flight. Linda was ready to give up and didn't know if we would even be let in the door in our current attire, and she was sure she would not be able to relax and enjoy the evening wearing a Cubs t-shirt, jeans, tennis shoes, and no makeup.

Paul Ruby and his wife Linda with Michael J. Fox

We then received some good news—our luggage would be delivered to our hotel and would arrive at about the same time that we were expected. We boarded the plane with a sense of relief. We had accepted the fact that we might be a few minutes late going to our hotel first, but we agreed attending the event dressed like Wrigley Field bleacher bums was not an option. The announcement from the captain that our takeoff was delayed thirty more minutes due to lightning resulted in another bout of tears. However, I was not ready to give up, and we couldn't get off the plane anyway, so I made a desperate call to the hotel. I explained my situation in detail to the concierge. The calm woman seemed to relish the challenge and asked me three questions at the end of our conversation: our budget, our sizes, and what brand of makeup did Linda wear?

Our taxi driver accepted my bribe and the challenge to get us to the restaurant on time and averted several potential accidents despite driving at unsafe speeds. We didn't know what to expect, but when we emerged from the Washington Tunnel, our cabbie assured us we would make our deadline. A few minutes later we arrived at the restaurant and saw the hotel's bellman waiting as promised holding two bags. After thanking him profusely, we changed into our new duds, one of us put makeup on, and we made our way to the reception to meet our host.

We had a wonderful experience thanks to the incredible service of the hotel staff. The amazing thing was the intention of my call to the hotel was simply to find out if there were any department stores near the restaurant. The concierge not only arranged for a personal shopper at the Century 21 department store but had first called the Michael J. Fox Foundation to confirm the attire for the evening.

We left New York with some new duds, a little less cash, and knowing how it feels when ordinary people are provided extraordinary service. If we return to New York, there is no doubt where we will stay . . . because we are now guests for life.

Rule 25: Don't let tacit approval become contagious.

Perception is reality in the hospitality industry. All staff are "on stage" all the time. This pertains to how other employees perceive us as well as guests. We can't afford to be inconsistent in the examples we set for those around us. We need to practice what we preach and never give our staff the opportunity to provide less than outstanding hospitality because they followed a bad example.

We must never become complacent and allow each other to set poor examples. The hotel should be treated as your home, with the desire to keep it clean and to be welcoming to anyone who enters.

At one time, we were having trouble with staff members taking too many smoke breaks. The breaks had become a social thing where multiple staff members, sometimes from the same department, were taking the breaks at the same time. This caused problems on a few levels so a policy was established that limited the number and duration of smoke breaks. The policy also specified that only one employee per department was allowed to be on break at any one time.

To add some bureaucracy to the process, anytime someone took a break they were required to put their name on sign-out sheet. This policy worked until one of the hotel supervisors felt he didn't need to put his name on the sheet. Once staff members saw that the supervisor was no longer signing out, they assumed that they no longer needed to.

Allowing compromises to continue only begets more compromises and can become a Petri dish for creating mediocrity.

Rule 26:
The fifteen—ten—five rule.

Focusing our attention on our guests is paramount. When an approaching guest is fifteen feet away, we should stop whatever we are doing and prepare to focus all our attention on the guest. When the person is within ten feet, we should be smiling and making eye contact with the guest to be approachable. When the guest is five feet away, proactively greet the guest, even if it is to tell them you will be with them in a moment. Our backs should never be turned to our guests.

Never underestimate the value of a smile. A warm and genuine smile creates a good first impression. A smile from a guest to an employee can suggest satisfaction or gratitude. A smile from an employee to a guest can show caring or appreciation. A smile from a supervisor to a line employee can signify a job well done. Smiles are positive. Smiles are always appreciated, and smiles can be contagious. It is said that a smile is the universal sign of kindness. Smiles are powerful!

"Let your smile change the world but don't let the world change your smile."

All businesses are faced from time to time with requests from customers that may seem impossible to fulfill. We typically manage our daily routines by following prescribed standard operating procedures that give employees an outline of how to handle recurring situations and standards to carry them out in a consistent manner. The problem is that often the most excellent customer service falls outside of the identified situation, frequently leaving employees without direction, or worse, giving employees the impression that it is okay to say no to a guest's request simply because they don't have a well-defined answer available. My approach throughout my years in hospitality, and life in general, has always been:

"Let's not focus on what we can't do, let's think about what we can do."

Initially employees will follow standard operating procedures after they've been trained to ensure a consistent and expected experience for our guests. It seems easy to just "play it by the book," until they begin to realize there isn't an answer in the book for every situation, nor should there be. The real key is for our staff's initial thought to always be "how can I provide exactly, if not more than, what the guest expects or needs?" Relying solely on reciting what is written in the standard operating procedure manual, only arms the staff with excuses for why we fail our guests.

Don't become standardized with the solutions to every opportunity that comes up. Fresh and innovative thinking will make a more lasting impression, and each guest may react differently in the same scenario. One guest may be thrilled with an apology call from the manager and an offer to change rooms in the case of an air conditioning problem, while it may take much more involved and creative efforts in order for the guest next door to leave with a good impression of the hotel.

Take responsibility in all that we do by using our best judgment, being timely and responsive, and following through to create closure. Be prompt and attentive. Procrastination and good service are not compatible. Returning an email or a phone call, getting back to guests in a timely manner is vital and typically within our control.

Sometimes a simple follow-up phone call to make sure housekeeping delivered the toothpaste the guest forgot shows that you truly care.

We all have an opportunity to make a positive impact on every guest who comes into the hotel. Our goal is to create a positive emotional connection with every patron to create guests for life.

Rule 27: Everyone's a Salesperson.

Regardless of one's title or position, we are all in sales. We may not all be involved with every part of the sales process, but we all can make an impact on closing some part of the deal. While some team members are rarely in a situation to bring in new business, that does not diminish their responsibility for helping to retain customers. We are not just selling hotel rooms, food, and drink. We are selling experiences.

Although customer service training typically revolves around front-of-the-house employees, the impact of staff who often has limited guest contact should never be underestimated. The extra detail on a garnish for a grilled cheese sandwich, a door being held open for a guest by a maintenance person, or simply a warm greeting by a room attendant, are all vital components of the desired culture within a hotel.

I had a wonderful experience at a hotel in Boston with my family. When one of my sons answered a knock on our guest room door, he was immediately greeted by the turndown attendant anxious to service our room. She had not met my boys before, but she had obviously memorized the names of the occupants prior to knocking as she proudly said, "Hello, Mr. Logan and Mr. Wes" upon entering. I was impressed not only by how well trained the staff were, but by the sincerity in the woman's eagerness to make my boys feel welcome and important.

This lovely woman was hired to clean rooms and turn down beds, but she clearly "sold" me on the hotel through her personal touch.

I was having lunch with Geneva's personable, outgoing, and some would say "comical" mayor when out of the blue he interrupted the couple at the table next to us to ask where they were from. This was the first time I had seen the thirty-something aged couple, who were enjoying what seemed to be a celebration luncheon. I cringed at the thought that the couple might not appreciate the mayor's assertiveness and wry sense of humor. But I soon began appreciating his ability to ingratiate himself, and by association, the hotel.

It was quickly determined that the couple was from Philadelphia, engaged to be married, had just been hired by a local company, and were on a search for a home in the area. They were staying at a competing hotel and thought they had narrowed their home search to a neighboring town. However, by the time the couple had walked out the door, they had switched hotels, had a new neighborhood to look at, and were dumbfounded by the mayor's Midwestern friendliness.

The couple ended up buying a house in Geneva, hosted a small party for their parents at the hotel, and are now regulars in the hotel's dining room. We will never know the full impact of this interaction as the couple continues to tell the story of the random encounter with the mayor and the hotel manager.

Encourage feedback from your staff. Create an environment where managers feel comfortable giving the boss constructive criticism without the fear of upsetting him or her. I recall my first Blackberry and how exciting it was when it would vibrate in my pocket to make me aware of a newly received email. I would instinctively retrieve the phone to see what was sent—often regardless of where I was or who I was with. I clearly had established a bad habit as one of my senior managers let me know that during staff meetings it appeared disrespectful when my attention veered away from those within the room and strayed to my phone. This has stuck with me, and I am grateful for the constructive criticism, and that my staff realized constructive criticism is healthy for everyone.

The Herrington has hosted dozens of A-list celebrities, including several heads of state, professional athletes, actors, and musicians. It is vital that guest confidentiality is never compromised and that the staff in theory treats celebrities no different than other guests. The bottom line is every guest should be treated like a VIP. The challenge is getting the staff to act like the hotel is used to having guests like Tom Hanks, Steve Martin, and Bob Dylan while remaining calm and not star struck by making these people feel like they are getting special attention.

Fuller's Car Wash/Service Center can consider me one of their customers for life. Their pricing isn't any better than their competition. My car doesn't end up cleaner than it does after any other car wash when they are done. However, the Fuller family gets it. There is a family member on-site at every one of their locations. The Fullers' aren't just keeping an eye on the staff and counting money; they are engaging with customers and developing personal connections whenever possible. They truly understand the concept of never letting customers do something that you can do for them.

From the owner loaning his personal vehicle so I can go back to work instead of waiting for an oil change, to taking my car to an unconnected muffler shop and ultimately saving me time and money, Fuller's makes things easy. I don't ask for these "favors." They are simply part of the service culture they have developed which separates them from the competition.

Mikhail Gorbachev had more than a few special requests during his three-night stay at the Herrington. The former Soviet Prime Minister requested bib lettuce, Roma tomatoes, olive oil, avocado, and cucumbers with a little sea salt before his steak. When he looked at the menu on his second visit to the hotel's dining room, he was delighted to find the "Gorbachev Salad" listed on the menu and with a proud beaming smile insisted that everyone in his entourage enjoy his contribution to the restaurant. While we can't name a menu item after every guest who has a special request, the goal is to create the perception that you would if you could.

Several years ago, William "The Refrigerator" Perry was in town having some dental work done. We had a beautiful suite on the third floor waiting for him. He saw the river behind the hotel and asked me if there were any fish in it. When I told him yes, he asked if he could switch to a first-floor room with a balcony overlooking the river. We made the room switch, and I made a call to a friend who was an avid fisherman who rushed over with a fishing pole and a bucket of minnows. I don't think The Fridge left the chair on his deck except to go to his dentist appointments. The former Chicago Bear was happy to show off the small-mouth bass he caught, as well as his smile and new teeth.

> **Rule 28:**
> Make each guest feel as though they are not only a VIP guest, but the hotel's only guest.

Focus on one customer at a time. Do what it takes to make the guest feel the hotel or restaurant is "their" hotel or restaurant. The importance in customer service of learning to focus completely and totally on one customer, even if only for a matter of seconds, is a vital component to instill in the staff.

I was preparing to host several Chinese dignitaries who came to Geneva to see the waste water treatment system used in one of the hotel owner's master planned communities. The system was being considered to be implemented in Beijing in preparation for the 2008

Summer Olympics. A dinner was planned to introduce the high-ranking Chinese to my boss and to the engineers who designed the cutting-edge technology I was also invited to the event and was charged with planning the intimate dinner party for twelve.

I wanted this event to be perfect, and I decided to invite the Chinese Consulate General in Chicago to the dinner. What was my motive for inviting him? The only thing I knew about proper protocol and etiquette in this type of situation was how easy it would be to offend our guests due to my ignorance of the Chinese culture. I was sure someone at the embassy would be able to help me not screw up.

It was a good thing I requested the crash course. Without it, I would have probably used white flowers on the table, which symbolize death; I would not have had gifts available to exchange with each dignitary; I would not have had Saki available for toasts; not known how to hand a business card, or how and when to bow. I also learned in advance the meaning of the word *ganbei*, which I was assured, would be used many times throughout the evening.

The dinner turned out to be a success, with no offending gestures or symbolism. The only thing I wish I had been prepared for was how to secretly dump what seemed like thirty toasts, or *ganbei*, without anyone noticing. In an effort to be polite, I paid the price the next morning with the worst hangover of my life.

One of the unlikeliest businesses I have been responsible for was a convenience store. Despite low margins and a limited customer base, the Mill Creek Market persevered, which I attribute to one person's ability to create a loyal customer base of regulars. These customers would religiously come in for their morning cup of joe and to see Kathy. Kathy is the world's most positive person. Her response to being asked how she is was an emphatic "fantastic!" She was always smiling. I have never heard anything negative come out of her mouth; she never missed a day of work and could be trusted completely. The best part was Kathy did not have to do anything special to create customers for life . . . she just had to be herself.

Regardless of what type of business we are managing, the common thread of striving to create loyalty by making an emotional connection between staff and customer will always be a priority.

Time to Make a Change

> **Rule 29:**
> *Stay connected.*

Over the years as my responsibilities grew and became more diversified, I started feeling that I was becoming further and further removed from many of the principles within this book.

My first clue was the number of stories about great customer service that I was either involved with or knew of firsthand had begun dwindling in proportion to my time spent out of my office. I also realized how important it was for my personal job satisfaction to be directly involved with achieving the hotel's mission statement.

I had become disconnected from that from which I drew inspiration, started showing signs of complacency, and was in jeopardy of not practicing what I was preaching. I decided to devote time each day interacting with guests and staff members. Fortunately, this simple change was not challenging or compromising, but instead rejuvenating.

There are hotel owners and general managers who rely entirely on analyzing a financial statement to determine whether a property is successful or not. It can be tough to find fault when the bottom line continues to improve. Some hotel owners and general managers are successful despite having little to no focus on customer service or possess a single drop of hospitality in their blood. You don't have to have a guest-centric personality to turn a profit in the hotel business. However, I don't know many "lifers" who don't find a significant portion of their job satisfaction from pleasing others and make maximizing customer service levels a very high priority in their properties.

There is a good reason every chain and most independent hotels track their guest service index. Service can and should be the ultimate differentiator. Good service gets guests to return. Great service gets guests to return and tell others. And when we bring service to a level where staff members make emotional connections, we have created guests for life.

Our goal is simple: develop a team and provide the tools, training, and empowerment to connect with our patrons on an emotional level in an effort to create guests for life. Achieving this goal may not guarantee we will meet our financial objectives, but when success is measured not only by red and black but also by our ability to provide consistent outstanding hospitality, we have improved the likelihood of success regardless of how it is defined.

It doesn't matter if we are a hotel general manager, an auto mechanic., or a bathroom attendant . . . we all have the ability to impact a customer's experience. The key is to embrace this ability and act by establishing emotional connections with the people we serve. Sometimes this entails resolving a complex problem, and sometimes it is as simple as providing a sincere greeting, a warm smile, and a clean towel.

I recently took the train from our home town of Geneva with my wife and two sons to Chicago. The purpose of our trip was to look at apartments for my oldest son Wes who had just graduated from college and would soon be starting his new job in the city.

For nostalgia sake, we decided to have lunch at the Berghoff before our first appointment. As we left the restaurant, I took a slight detour. All four of us were in need of a restroom, and I directed our group through an unmarked door on State Street that took us inside a retail area adjacent to the Palmer House. We proceeded to the lower level where the restrooms were located just as my father had done forty-some years earlier.

I didn't know what to expect as we approached the men's room with my two sons. Wes and Logan had heard the story of the men's room attendant many times, and they knew why we had gone out of our way to use this particular restroom. Upon entering, I sensed my sons felt some of the disappointment that I was experiencing as we were alone and the men's room attendant had been replaced by an automatic paper towel dispenser.

As we joined my wife and headed up the escalator to the lobby, I wondered if I were a young boy now what kind of experience would it take to inspire me to want to be a hotelier?

The answer in my head was not immediately apparent. But as I reminisced about the men's room attendant who had provided me and thousands of others a warm greeting and a clean towel, I realized that I have never forgotten how this one individual had made me feel.

This feeling did not come from a building or a function within a hotel. The unforgettable feeling of complete satisfaction could only come from a person whose desire to serve others transcended everything else in their quest to "create guests for life."

Ruby's Rules

Rule 1: Surround yourself with good people.

Rule 2: Keep things fun.

Rule 3: Inspect what you expect.

Rule 4: Treat those you are serving in the manner in which you would like to be treated.

Rule 5: Don't let training be an excuse for compromised service.

Rule 6: Follow up on feedback.

Rule 7: All team members must be empowered to make decisions.

Rule 8: Do it right the first time.

Rule 9: Mind your manners.

Rule 10: When "no means no;" and when it means an opportunity lost.

Rule 11: Adversity creates opportunity.

Rule 12: The guest is not always right, but they are still our guest and need to stay that way.

Rule 13: Patience is more than a virtue. It's also a customer service necessity.

Rule 14: To be or not to be . . . Be assuring, sincere, and eager to please. Don't be unsure, presumptuous, or untimely.

Ruby's Rules

Rule 15: Sometimes you need to accept the fact that you can't make everyone happy and there are some guests who are better off being someone else's problem.

Rule 16: Solicit guest feedback and respond when you get it.

Rule 17: Anticipate, follow-up, and be proactive.

Rule 18: Focus on what we can control.

Rule 19: See and experience what guests see and experience.

Rule 20: Create a memorable experience.

Rule 21: Know how to make a guest feel special.

Rule 22: Keep thorough records.

Rule 23: When is it okay to assume?

Rule 24: Never leave a guest to do something for themselves that you can do for them.

Rule 25: Don't let tacit approval become contagious.

Rule 26: The fifteen—ten—five rule.

Rule 27: Everyone's a Salesperson.

Rule 28: Make each guest feel as though they are not only a VIP guest, but the hotel's only guest.

Rule 29: Stay connected.

Acknowledgments

Thank you to Dawn Vogelsberg for her Contributions. Without Dawn's involvement, this project would never have been finished . . . she also took care of the things I dislike doing.

Thank you to one of my oldest friends, Jay Harrison, for providing his editing skills.

I am grateful to Dr. Thomas Walsh for his thirty-five years of mentoring and to Dave Flando for preparing me to fill his shoes at the Drake.

Thank you to Henry Czapla for always being a great example.

I am thankful to my parents for providing me so many opportunities, and to Linda, Wes, and Logan for putting up with my obsessive behaviors.

Thank you to Rene Boer and Scott Lebin for their advice and unwavering positive attitudes.

I am grateful to the Shodeen family for creating the Herrington and allowing me to be its innkeeper for the past twenty years. And thanks most of all to the countless managers and line employees I have worked with, counted on and learned from during the past thirty-five years.

About the Author

**PAUL RUBY
President,
Shodeen Hospitality**

**General Manger,
Herrington Inn & Spa**

A veteran of the hospitality industry, Paul Ruby notes a thirty-year career distinguished by management positions at such respected properties as the Palmer House Hotel and Towers in Chicago, the Drake Hotel in Oakbrook, Illinois, Lake Shore Country Club in Glencoe, Illinois, and the Herrington Inn & Spa in Geneva, Illinois.

Paul holds a Bachelor of Science in Hotel and Restaurant Management from Iowa State University. His entrepreneurial interests include the development and operation of businesses including, "Ruby's On the Park," "T.F. Boonies Saloon & Eatery," "Tanna Farms Golf Club," and "The Mill Creek Market" as well as consulting for several Chicago area restaurant ventures.

Paul got his start within Hilton Hotels and became the Front Desk Manager for Chicago's oldest hotel, the prominent 1,700-room Palmer House Hotel and Towers. He soon was tapped for a position at the Drake Oakbrook Hotel where he was eventually promoted to General Manager.

Paul left the Drake to open up his own restaurant in the Lincoln Park Neighborhood of Chicago. He designed, built, and operated "Ruby's on the Park," a white table cloth restaurant located across from the Lincoln Park Zoo.

Paul spent three seasons as Clubhouse Manager at Lake Shore Country Club where he fine-tuned his luxury service skills.

Since 1999, Paul Ruby has served as the General Manager of the sixty-one room Herrington Inn & Spa, a AAA Four-Diamond-hotel for twenty-five consecutive years. Paul was promoted in 2008 to Vice President of Operations and became President of Shodeen Hospitality in 2015. He oversees the operations of several businesses including golf courses, a banquet facility, and two limited service hotels in addition to his responsibilities as General Manager of the Herrington.

In 2006 Paul was diagnosed with Parkinson's disease. He founded the Paul Ruby Foundation for Parkinson's Research in 2007, and in the organization's first year was honored as the largest Team Fox fundraiser in the country benefiting the Michael J. Fox Foundation. In 2008 the PRF affiliated with the Movement Disorder Center at Northwestern Hospital in Chicago. The foundation raised over $1,000,000 for Parkinson's disease research before it was dissolved in 2014.

Paul has served on several boards including the Iowa State University Alumni Association, the Geneva Economic Commission, the Geneva Chamber of Commerce, and the Geneva Baseball Association. Paul received the American Red Cross Hometown Hero Award in 2006 for his efforts relating to assisting Hurricane Katrina victims.

Paul was born August 7, 1963. He is married to Linda Ruby. They have two children: Wesley, age twenty-two, and Logan, age nineteen.

www.ingramcontent.com/pod-product-compliance
Lightning Source LLC
Chambersburg PA
CBHW071520080526
44588CB00011B/1507